LONGMAN

PHOTO DICTIONARY

PEARSON

Longman **NEW EDITION**

CONTENTS

CONTENTS

PERSONAL DATA

1 name
2 surname/family name
3 first name
4 initials
5 age
6 sex
7 marital status
8 date of birth
9 place of birth
10 country of birth
11 next of kin
12 address
13 postcode
14 telephone number
15 e-mail address
16 single
17 married
18 divorced
19 widow/widower

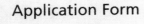

Application Form

Please complete all of the items on the form to the best of your knowledge. Use blue or black ink only.

Application for — Sales Manager
Surname (1) — Smith (2)
First Name — John (3)   Initials (4) — JS

Age (5) 25   Sex (6) *male* ☑ female ○ (please tick)

Marital Status (7)   single ☑   married ○   divorced ○
                          widow/widower ○

Date of Birth (8) 7 May 1976   Place of Birth (9) Bristol
Country of Birth (10) United Kingdom
Next of Kin (11) Susan Smith

Address — 23 Southfield Road, Purbey, Westshire (12)
Postcode (13) PU23 4HJ
Telephone — 0560 152439 (14)

E-mail address (15) jsmith@internetsp.com

Qualifications — 6 GCSEs and 3 A-levels (see CV for details)

Previous Employment — GRM logistics, Monkbridge, 1995 – present
Sam's Newsagents, Purbey (part-time) only, 1993-5

20 child
21 baby
22 toddler
23 teenager
24 adult
25 elderly (old)

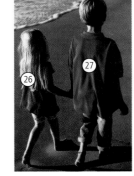

26 girl
27 boy
28 man
29 woman

What's your postcode?
It's SN11 3BJ.

What's your marital status?
I'm married./I'm a widower.

A: **What's your marital status?**
B: I'm ....

A: **What's your** ....?
B: It's/I'm (a) ....

Questions for discussion
1 Give the personal data of someone you know.
2 Give the personal data of a famous person.

wife and husband:
2 and 1; 5 and 6; 3 and 11

ex-wife and ex-husband:
3 and 4; 12 and 11

father and son:
1 and 6; 4 and 8; 6 and 10; 11 and 14, 15

mother and daughter:
2 and 3; 3 and 7, 13; 5 and 9; 12 and 16

brother and sister:
3 and 6; 7 and 8; 9 and 10; 13 and 14;
15 and 16

sisters-in-law:
3 and 5

brothers-in-law:
6 and 11

father-in-law and son-in-law:
1 and 11

mother-in-law and daughter-in-law:
2 and 5

parent(s) and child(ren):
1, 2 and 3, 6; 3, 4 and 7, 8; 5, 6 and 9, 10;
11, 12 and 15, 16; 11, 3 and 13, 14

grandparents and grandchildren:
1, 2 and 7, 8, 9, 10, 13, 14

grandfather and grandson:
1 and 8, 10, 14

grandmother and granddaughter:
2 and 7, 9, 13

uncle and nephew:
6 and 8, 14

aunt and niece:
5 and 7, 13; 3 and 9

cousins:
7, 8 and 9, 10

single parent:
12

remarried
3 and 11

stepfather and stepdaughter:
11 and 7

stepmother and stepson:
3 and 15

stepbrother and stepsister:
8 and 16; 15 and 7

half-brother and half-sister:
15 and 13; 14 and 16; 14 and 7; 8 and 13

① Robert Elliot ② Ann Elliot

③ Sue Elliot ④ Peter Blackburn ⑤ Elaina Elliot (née Kim) ⑥ Tim Elliot

⑦ Emily Blackburn ⑧ Jack Blackburn ⑨ Tessa Elliot ⑩ Chris Elliot

③ Sue Elliot ⑪ John Murray ⑫ Anna Murray

⑬ Sophie Elliot-Murray ⑭ Daniel Elliot-Murray ⑮ Stephen Murray ⑯ Rosie Murray

⎍⎍⎍⎍ Shows that people are divorced

Who's she? (5)
She's Tessa's mother.

Who's he? (8)
He's Tim's nephew.

A: Who's she? (3)
B: ....

A: Who's he/she?
B: He/She's ....'s ....

Questions for discussion
1 Which of these words apply to women?
2 Which of these words can be used for men and women?
3 Draw your family tree and describe it.

DAILY ROUTINE/HOME ACTIVITIES

1 wake up
2 get up
3 have a shower
4 shave
5 dry yourself
6 brush your teeth
7 wash your face
8 rinse your face

9   get dressed
10 comb your hair
11 put on make-up
12 eat breakfast
13 have a cup of coffee

14 go to work
15 watch (TV)
16 listen to the radio
17 read (the paper)
18 have a bath
19 brush your hair
20 go to bed
21 sleep

Is she getting up? (2)
Yes, she is.

Is he having a shower? (18)
No, he isn't. He's having a bath.

A: **Is she listening to the radio? (15)**
B: ....

A: **Is he/she** ....?
B: Yes, he/she is./No, he/she isn't.

Questions for discussion
1 Which of these things do you do in the morning?
2 In which order do you do them?
3 Which of these things do you do in the evening?

A DETACHED HOUSE
1 porch
2 garage
3 front garden, yard *AmE*
4 drive

B TERRACED HOUSES
5 gate
6 fence

C FRONT DOOR
7 knocker
8 doorknob
9 letterbox
10 front door
11 doorbell
12 doorstep

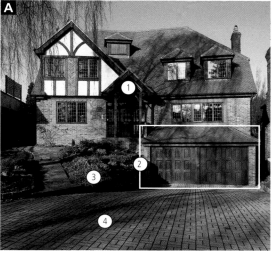

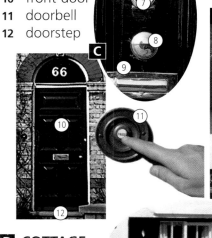

D COTTAGE
13 chimney
14 shutter
15 window

E FLATS
16 balcony

F SEMI-DETACHED HOUSE
17 TV aerial

G BUNGALOW
18 gutter   20 roof
19 satellite dish 21 drainpipe

Do you live in a detached house?
Yes, I do./No, I don't.

A: Do you live in a flat?
B: ....

A: **Do you live in a** ....?
B: Yes, I do./No, I don't.

Questions for discussion
1 Which of these places to live are common in your country? Where do you find them?
2 Describe your home.

1 tap, faucet *AmE*
2 sink
3 drawer
4 double oven
5 kitchen unit
6 cupboard
7 (cooking) pot
8 work-surface/worktop

9 hob
10 hotplate
11 (door) handle

12 dishwasher
13 bin
14 (aluminium) foil
15 clingfilm™

16 fridge/refrigerator
17 freezer
18 cafetiere
19 cookery book
20 storage jar
21 spices
22 spice rack

23 washing-up liquid
24 dishcloth
25 tea towel

Where's the cupboard?
It's on the wall.

Where are the spices?
They're in the spice rack.

A: **Where's the fridge?**
B: It's .... the ....

A: **Where's/Where are the** ....?
B: It's/They're on/next to/in the ....

Questions for discussion
1 Which of these things are used for storage?
2 Which of these things are used for preparing food?
3 Which of these things are used for washing or cleaning things?

1 lid
2 wok
3 handle
4 chopping board
5 knife
6 food processor
7 microwave
8 casserole dish
9 roasting tin
10 cake tin
11 oven glove
12 baking tray
13 steamer
14 peeler
15 sieve
16 garlic press
17 toaster
18 (hand) beater/
   rotary whisk

19 blender
20 rolling pin
21 tin opener
22 ladle

23 kettle
24 measuring spoon
25 grater
26 (mixing) bowl
27 whisk
28 measuring jug
29 (electric) mixer
30 bottle opener
31 coffee maker
32 saucepan
33 frying pan

What do you do with a whisk?
You beat eggs or cream with it.

What do you do with a roasting tin?
You roast meat in it.

A: **What do you do with
   a ....?**
B: You .... in/with it.

Questions for discussion
Which of these things do you need to make:
1 a cheese omelette?
2 a cake?

1 bath
2 bath mat
3 tile
4 toilet
5 shower
6 mug
7 toothpaste
8 toothbrush
9 toothbrush holder
10 razor
11 shaving gel
12 shaving brush
13 soap

14 soap dish
15 soap dispenser
16 mirror
17 shelf
18 hot water tap
19 cold water tap
20 washbasin
21 toilet roll

22 laundry basket
23 bath towel
24 hand towel
25 towel rail
26 shower curtain
27 bathroom cabinet
28 shampoo
29 shower gel
30 conditioner
31 facecloth/flannel

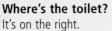

Where's the toilet?
It's on the right.

Where's the washbasin?
It's on the left.

Where's the bath mat?
It's in the middle.

A: Where's/Where are the ....?
B: It's/They're on the right/on the left/in the middle.

Questions for discussion
1 How long do you spend in the bathroom each day? Why?
2 Do you prefer having a bath or a shower? Why?

1 chest of drawers
2 drawer
3 handle
4 lamp
5 bedside table
6 wallpaper
7 (scatter) cushion
8 double bed
9 carpet
10 pillowcase
11 pillow
12 alarm clock
13 headboard
14 bedspread
15 single bed
16 blanket
17 sheet
18 (fitted) sheet
19 duvet/quilt
20 valance

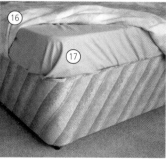

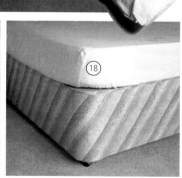

21 mirror
22 dressing table
23 wardrobe
24 mattress
25 radiator

Where's the mattress?
It's underneath the sheets.

Where are the cushions?
They're on top of the duvet.

A: **Where's the lamp?**
B: It's .... the ....

A: **Where's/Where are the** ....?
B: It's/They're underneath/on top of the ....

Questions for discussion
1 What was your bedroom like when you were little?
2 What is your bedroom like now?

1	window	**10**	plant pot/tub	**19**	fireplace
2	curtain, drape *AmE*	**11**	armchair	**20**	fireguard
3	picture frame	**12**	cushion	**21**	writing table
4	picture	**13**	coffee table	**22**	remote control
5	lampshade	**14**	flowers	**23**	television
6	lamp	**15**	vase	**24**	video recorder
7	bookcase	**16**	sofa/settee		
8	books	**17**	rug		
9	plant	**18**	mantelpiece		

Are there any curtains in your living room?
Yes, there are.

Is there a bookcase in your living room?
No, there isn't.

A: Are there any/Is there a/an
.... **in your living room?**

B: Yes there are./No there aren't./
Yes, there is./No, there isn't.

Questions for discussion

1 Which of these things are soft?

2 Do living rooms in your country look like this? What is different?

1 side table
2 chair
3 (dining room) table
4 candle
5 teapot
6 cake stand
7 place mat
8 salt
9 pepper
10 serving dish
11 serviette/napkin
12 serviette/napkin ring
13 tray
14 coaster

A CROCKERY

15 jug
16 wine glass
17 cup
18 saucer
19 bowl
20 plate

B CUTLERY

21 fork
22 knife
23 dessertspoon
24 teaspoon
25 soup spoon

Where's the pepper?
It's to the right of the salt.

Where's the fork? (B)
It's to the left of the knife.

A: Where's the ....?
B: It's .... of the
   ....

Questions for discussion
1 Which of these things are used for serving food?
2 Which of these things do you use for drinking?

1 teat
2 (baby) bottle
3 (baby) cup
4 (box of) tissues
5 dummy
6 mobile
7 soft toy
8 teddy bear
9 cot
10 baby carrier
11 sterilizer
12 potty
13 (baby) wipes
14 changing mat
15 nappy
16 car seat

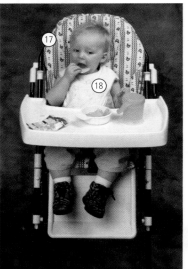

17 high chair
18 bib
19 bouncer
20 pushchair (buggy)
21 pram
22 (baby) clothes
23 intercom

Where's the baby? (16)
He's in his car seat.

Where's the baby? (9)
She's in her cot.

A: Where's the baby?
B: He's/She's in/on his/her
....

Questions for discussion

1 Which of these things can a baby sit or lie in?

2 Which of these things are used for feeding a baby?

1 clothesline/washing line
2 peg
3 fabric conditioner
4 iron
5 socket
6 plug
7 duster
8 dustpan
9 brush
10 ironing board
11 sponge mop

12 broom/brush
13 mop
14 bucket

15 laundry basket
16 airer
17 washing powder
18 washing machine
19 tumble dryer
20 vacuum cleaner
21 scrubbing brush
22 coat hanger

Where's the iron?
It's on the ironing board.

Where's the laundry?
It's in the laundry basket.

A: **Where's the mop?**
B: It's .... the ....

A: **Where's the** ....?
B: It's in/on the ....

Questions for discussion
1 Do you do any housework in your house?
2 Which jobs do you do?
3 How often do you use these things?

1 umbrella/parasol
2 patio
3 (patio) chair
4 (patio) table
5 flowerbed
6 lawn
7 pond
8 sun lounger
9 barbecue
10 bush
11 garden shed
12 tree
13 greenhouse
14 hedge
15 swing
16 vegetable garden
17 border

FLOWERS

18 lily
19 pansy
20 tulip
21 petunia
22 geranium
23 iris
24 chrysanthemum
25 daffodil
26 hyacinth
27 snapdragon
28 daisy
29 orchid
30 rose

Where's the pond?
It's next to the lawn, to the left of the bridge.

Where's the tree?
It's on the lawn, to the right of the shed.

A: **Where's the swing?**
B: It's ....

A: **Where's the** ....?
B: It's ....

Questions for discussion
1 Do you have a garden?
2 What are your favourite flowers?
3 Describe your ideal garden.

1 lawn mower
2 watering can
3 seeds
4 seed trays
5 hedge trimmer
6 secateurs
7 shears
8 gardening gloves
9 trowel
10 slug pellets
11 potting shed
12 compost
13 rake
14 fork
15 spade
16 wheelbarrow
17 fence
18 pot/tub
19 hose/hosepipe
20 fertiliser
21 tap

SLUG
MINI-PELLETS
SHOWER PROOF

WITH SPECIAL
ANIMAL REPELLENT

22 sprinkler
23 tie up a branch
24 dig the soil
25 water the plants
26 plant flowers
27 weed the flowerbed
28 prune a shrub
29 mow the lawn

A: **I want to water the garden.**
B: You need a watering can or a sprinkler.

A: **I want to cut some roses.**
B: You need secateurs.

A: **I want to** ....
B: You need (a) ....
   and/or (a) ....

Questions for discussion
1 Do you like gardening?
2 Which of these things do you do?

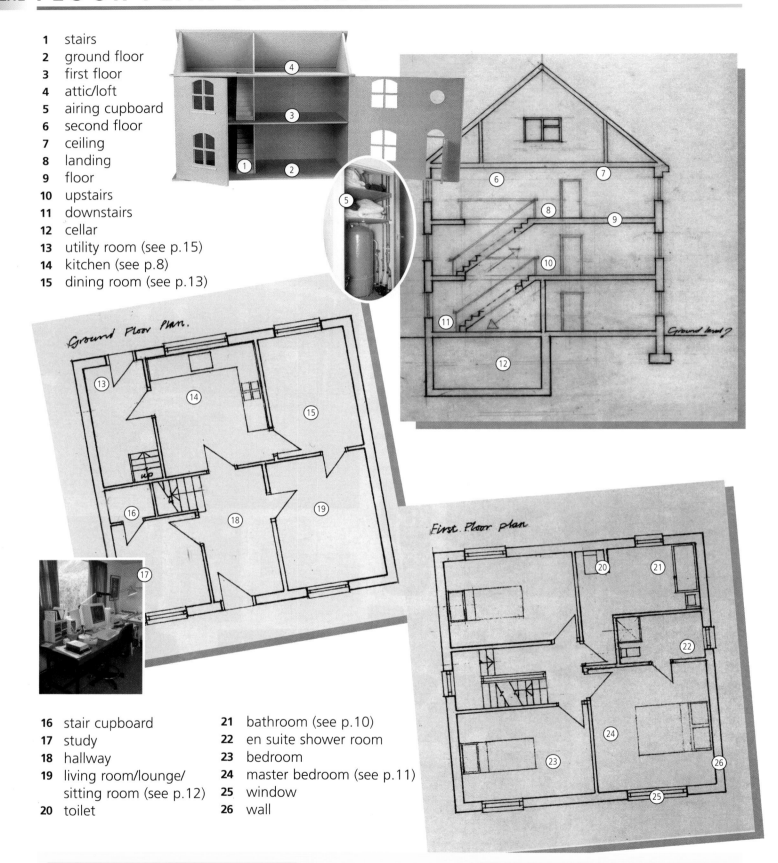

1 stairs
2 ground floor
3 first floor
4 attic/loft
5 airing cupboard
6 second floor
7 ceiling
8 landing
9 floor
10 upstairs
11 downstairs
12 cellar
13 utility room (see p.15)
14 kitchen (see p.8)
15 dining room (see p.13)

16 stair cupboard
17 study
18 hallway
19 living room/lounge/ sitting room (see p.12)
20 toilet

21 bathroom (see p.10)
22 en suite shower room
23 bedroom
24 master bedroom (see p.11)
25 window
26 wall

Has your home got a cellar/dining room?
Yes, it has./No, it hasn't.

How many bedrooms has your home got?
It's got two.

A: **How many .... has your home got?**
B: It's got ....

Questions for discussion
1 Which of these things do you have in your home?
2 Which of these things are common in homes in your country?

1 make the bed
2 make breakfast
3 feed the dog
4 take the children to school
5 take the bus to school

6 hoover/vacuum
7 sweep
8 wash the floor
9 dust
10 iron
11 sew
12 feed the baby
13 wash the dishes
14 load the dishwasher
15 pick up the children

16 walk the dog
17 go shopping
18 cook/make lunch/dinner
19 do the laundry
20 study
21 do homework

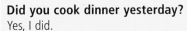

Did you cook dinner yesterday?
Yes, I did.

Did you do the laundry yesterday?
No, I didn't.

A: **Did you go shopping yesterday?**
B: ....

A: **Did you** .... **yesterday?**
B: Yes, I did./No, I didn't.

Questions for discussion
1 Which of these activities do you do every day?
2 Which activities do you like/dislike?

19

1 CV, résumé *AmE*
2 interview
3 application form
4 covering letter
5 telephone number
6 fax number
7 e-mail
8 job adds
9 job board

① **Curriculum Vitae**

Name	John Smith
Address	23 Southfield Road Purbey Westshire PU23 4HJ
Age	25
Date of Birth	7 May 1976
Marital Status	Single
Occupation	Sales Assistant
Education	Purbey Comprehensive School 1988-95
Qualifications	GCSE Mathematics B English B Geography A History B French C Art B A-levels Business studies B English C French D
Employment	*Customer services assistant – GRM Logistic...* My first job involved dealing with custome... post. I also helped run the customer data... for sales managers. I had to be well organ... needs. *Sales assistant – GRM Logistics* I directly supported the sales manager in... handled some accounts without supervisi... when necessary. Good negotiating and c... essential.
Other Interests	Outside of work I am a member of the lo... Saturday this also includes two nights fo... I also play the drums in a band and we h... clubs about three times a month.

②

④

John Smith
23 Southfield Road
Purbey
Westshire PU23 4HJ
⑤ Telephone   0560 152439
⑥ Fax   0560 256439

Dear Sir/Madam,

I am writing to apply for the position of Sales Manager advertised in The Evening Post on 24 August 2000.

I have been working for the past two years as a sales assistant within a busy department. I believe this has given me excellent experience and the confidence to take a step forward in my career.

As requested I enclose my full CV and application form. If there is any other information you require, please don't hesitate to contact me.

I look forward to your reply.

Yours sincerely,

John Smith

③ **Application Form**

Application for	Sales Manager
Surname	Smith
First Name	John
Age	25
Marital Status	single ☑ m... widow/widower ○
Date of Birth	7 May 1976
Country of Birth	United Kingdom
Next of Kin	Susan Smith
Address	23 Southfield Road, Purbey, Westshire
Postcode	PU23 4HJ
Telephone	0560 152439
⑦ E-mail address	jsmith@internetsp.com
Qualifications	6 GCSEs and 3 A-levels (see CV for details)
Previous Employment	GRM logistics, Monkbridge, 1995 – present Sam's Newsagents, Purbey (part-time) only, 1993-5

17 The Evening Post 24 August 2000

⑧ **Recruitment 01432 56 73 99**

The Evening Post Jobfinder

WE ARE LOOKING for a reception / administration assistant for three days a week. Basic knowledge of computers and typing required. Call GH & M Solicitors on 01635 2673872

CARPENTERS REQUIRED for local contracts. £650 pw. Long run of work avail... ...st be a member ...r Guild or similar ...onal body. Tele- ...1722 872 2536

...STANT wanted ...l for Spring ...nt school ...rest in a ...ideal. ...342

TEMPING. Give us a call now. Excellent opportunities in this area. AJJ Recruitment 0800 263 3677.

Domestic

CLEANERS required for city centre office. Monday to Friday, 6-8am. £5 per hour. Please phone 467 3927 (during office hours).

EARLY MORNING CLEANING people wanted. Must be punctual. 6.30am start. £4 ph. Saturday to Wednesday. Telephone Mr Jones on 01643 2536732.

WINDOW CLEANER wanted for established round. Will consider school-leaver. ...

RECEPTIONIST required for a busy dental surgery. Two days a week for 6 months to cover maternity leave. Must have experience. Telephone J Brown Dental Surgery on 01523 467 3764

LOOKING for an exciting challenge? Get into telesales. £14k pa starting pay. To rise following assessment. Great prospects for the right candidate. 01643 4673763.

PART-TIME assistant wanted for Newsagents. Must be able to work mornings. Tel. 233223. Ask for Jim.

DOMESTIC HELP wanted. Two days a week. For more information ... 3452

PERSON required to assist moving contractors. Must be strong and fit. Heavy lifting involved. Phone 01534 362 8373

EXPERIENCED Bricklayers and plumbers wanted for new housing development in city centre. Good pay rates. Must have hat and boots. Contact Bill Simmons — Tel 04536 63656.

Hotel & Catering

BAR STAFF wanted for The Swan Public House, Barfield Way. Experience essential. Various hours available, fun and friendly people need only apply. — contact Tim or Rose on 04537 266 7366

CHEF required for village restaurant. Great rates of pay. 20 hours per week at £5.25 per hour. Must have relevant professional qualifications. — Telephone Mavis on 423 323.

SAM'S SANDWICHS need a sandwich maker. Would suit student. Early hours. Tel. 01332 4333332

BAR STAFF required for local public house. Sense of humour essential. £3.50 per hour evenings and weekends available. Tel. 345233 after 3pm

SKILLED bar people wanted for nightclub. Fridays and Saturdays only. 9pm-2am. £4.25 per hour...

⑨ **Vacancies**

What should you include in a CV?
You should include your qualifications and work experience.

A: What should you send with an application form?
B: You should send ....

A: Where should you look if you want to find a new job?
B: You should look ....

Questions for discussion
1 Do you have a job?
2 How did you find your job?

1 farmer
2 baker
3 mechanic
4 taxi driver
5 electrician
6 lorry driver
7 soldier
8 florist
9 window cleaner
10 carpenter

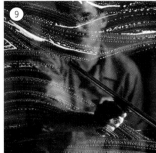

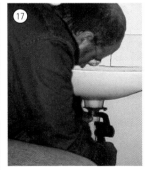

11 chef/cook
12 painter
13 waiter
14 bricklayer
15 gardener
16 greengrocer
17 plumber
18 refuse collector
19 fisherman
20 butcher
21 motorcycle courier

Who do you think has the most difficult job?
A chef.

A: Who do you think has the most
.... job/the ....est job?
B: A/An ....

Questions for discussion
Choose three jobs:
1 Do you know anyone that does these jobs?
2 What qualities do you need for these jobs?

1 vet, veterinarian *AmE*
2 nurse
3 doctor
4 pharmacist
5 fire fighter
6 scientist
7 optician
8 dentist
9 barrister/lawyer
10 judge
11 postman/postwoman
12 police officer
13 lecturer
14 teacher
15 nursery assistant

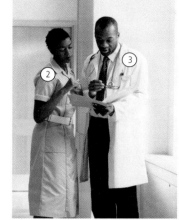

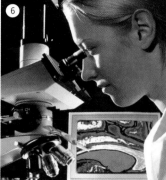
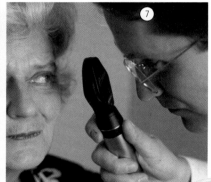

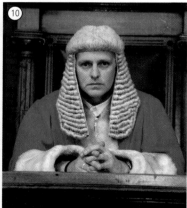

Who do you think has the most interesting job?
A scientist.

A: Who do you think has the most .... job/the ....est job?
B: A/An ....

Questions for discussion

Choose three jobs:

1 Do you know anyone that does these jobs?
2 What qualities do you need for these jobs?

1 journalist
2 newsreader
3 secretary/personal assistant (PA)
4 computer technician
5 accountant
6 sales assistant
7 estate agent
8 financial adviser
9 travel agent
10 bank clerk

11 receptionist
12 factory worker/blue-collar worker
13 office worker/white-collar worker
14 telemarketing executive
15 photographer
16 hairdresser
17 artist
18 draughtsman
19 architect
20 designer

Would you like to be a photographer?
Yes, I would.
No, I wouldn't.

A: **Would you like to be a newsreader?**
B: ....

A: **Would you like to be a/an** ....?
B: Yes, I would./No, I wouldn't.

Questions for discussion
Which of the jobs on the last three pages:
1 involve hard physical work?
2 are creative?

1 desk tidy
2 calendar
3 noticeboard
4 electric typewriter
5 (desk) lamp
6 computer
7 desk
8 swivel chair
9 telephone
10 in tray
11 out tray
12 files
13 paper clip holder
14 paper clips
15 desk diary
16 Sellotape™
17 correction fluid/
   Tipp-Ex™ *BrE*
18 Post-it™ notes

19 notepad
20 (ballpoint) pen/biro™
21 hole-punch
22 stapler
23 fax machine
24 franking machine
25 photocopier
26 pencils
27 elastic band/rubber band
28 rubber
29 wastepaper basket/bin

Why do people use files?
They use them to store documents in.

A: **Why do people use correction fluid?**
B: They use it to ....

A: **Why do people use** ....?
B: They use them/it to ....

Questions for discussion
1 Which items need electricity?
2 Which items fix things together?
3 Which items do you have in your house?

1 take notes
2 type a letter
3 staple documents together
4 fill in a form
5 sign a letter
6 note appointments
7 file papers
8 filing cabinet
9 photocopy a letter
10 send a fax/fax a document
11 answer the phone
12 print a hard copy
13 greet visitors
14 offer refreshments
15 write a memo
16 send an e-mail

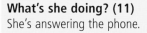

What's she doing? (11)
She's answering the phone.

What's he doing? (15)
He's writing a memo.

A: **What's he doing? (9)**
B: He's ....

A: **What's he/she doing?**
B: He's/She's ....

Questions for discussion

1 Which of these activities would a manager do?
2 Which of these activities would an assistant do?
3 Which of these activities are boring?

1 mallet
2 toolbox
3 tape measure
4 hand saw
5 hacksaw
6 power saw
7 Stanley knife™
8 hammer
9 nails
10 screwdriver
11 screws
12 nut
13 bolt
14 washer

15 workbench
16 plane
17 sandpaper
18 chisel
19 vice

20 hatchet/axe
21 bradawl
22 square
23 power/electric drill
24 (drill) bits
25 pliers
26 (adjustable) spanner
27 file
28 wrench
29 paintbrush
30 (paint) pot
31 hook
32 (paint) tray
33 (paint) roller
34 paint

What's this? (23)
It's a power drill.

What are these? (31)
They're hooks.

A: **What's this?/What are these?**
B: It's a/They're.. .

Questions for discussion

Which things would you need if you wanted to:

1 make a table?

2 paint your bedroom?

26

1. (assembly) line
2. machine
3. worker
4. work station
5. time clock
6. time card
7. forklift
8. pallet

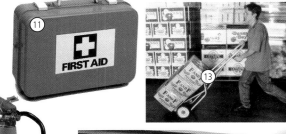

9. conveyor belt
10. safety goggles
11. first-aid kit
12. fire extinguisher
13. hand truck
14. warehouse
15. loading dock/bay
16. freight lift
17. foreman

FIRST AID

What are time cards?
They're cards that show how many hours a worker works.

What's a warehouse?
It's a place where things are stored.

A: What are ....?/What's a ....?
B: They're/It's a .... that/where ....

Questions for discussion

1. Which of these objects are used for carrying things?
2. Which of these things are necessary for safety?

ON A CONSTRUCTION SITE

1 crane
2 scaffolding
3 ladder
4 construction worker
5 hard hat
6 tool belt
7 girder
8 hook
9 excavation site
10 dumper truck
11 cement mixer
12 cement
13 digger/excavator
14 ear protectors/defenders
15 wheelbarrow
16 pneumatic drill
17 brick
18 trowel
19 bulldozer
20 sledgehammer
21 two-way radio
22 spirit level
23 pickaxe
24 shovel

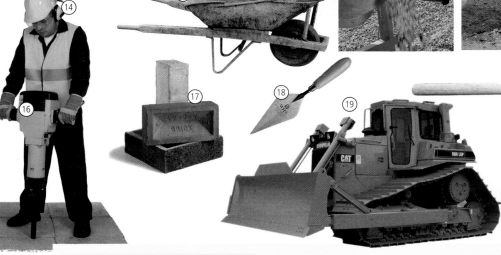

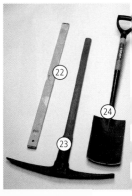

Have you ever used a pickaxe?
Yes, I have.

Have you ever worn a hard hat?
No, I haven't.

A: **Have you ever used/worn a**
.........................?
B: Yes, I have./No, I haven't.

Questions for discussion
1 Which of these things do people drive?
2 Which of these things make a lot of noise?
3 Which of these things could a person carry?

1 three-star hotel
2 chambermaid
3 foyer
4 checking in
5 checking out
6 receptionist
7 guest
8 reception
9 bar
10 restaurant

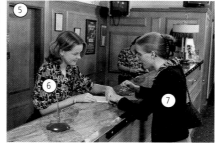

11 lift, elevator *AmE*
12 porter
13 suitcase
14 double room
15 bathroom
16 twin room
17 room key

18 trouser press
19 room service
20 newspaper
21 conference room

wrong Fergie

I'd like a twin room, please.
Certainly, sir.

I'd like to check out, please.
Certainly, madam.

A: **I'd like a/to**
...................., **please.**

B: ....

Questions for discussion

What is the difference between:

1 checking in and checking out?
2 a twin room and a double room?

1 suspect
2 police officer
3 handcuffs
4 evidence
5 courtroom
6 witness
7 court reporter
8 judge
9 barrister
10 jury
11 defendant
12 guard

13 solicitor
14 prison
15 prison officer
16 inmate
17 verdict

Who helps a crime suspect?
A solicitor.

Who listens to the evidence in a courtroom?
The judge and jury.

A: **Who gives evidence in a courtroom?**
B: A ....

A: **Who** ....?
B: A/The ....

Questions for discussion

1 Is the legal system in your country the same as this?

2 Are there any crime series on TV in your country?

3 What jobs do people in these TV series do?

1 head
2 arm
3 back
4 waist
5 buttocks
6 leg
7 face
8 chest
9 stomach
10 hip
11 hand
12 foot
13 eye
14 nose
15 mouth
16 chin
17 hair
18 ear
19 lips
20 neck

21 nail
22 thumb
23 finger
24 wrist

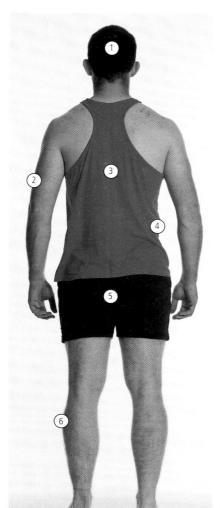

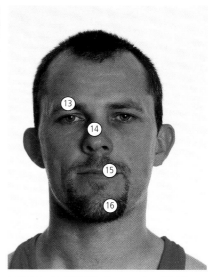
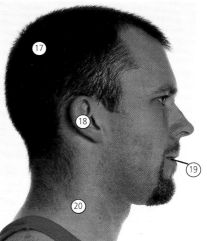
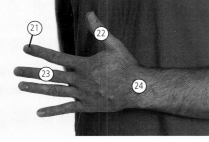
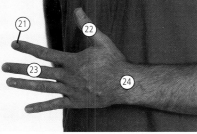

25 palm
26 shoulder
27 forearm
28 upper arm
29 elbow

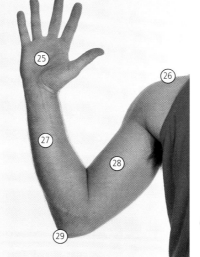
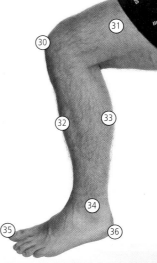

30 knee
31 thigh
32 shin
33 calf
34 ankle
35 toe
36 heel

Have you ever broken your wrist?
Yes, I broke it a few years ago.

Have you ever injured your back?
No, never.

A: **Have you ever broken your ankle?**
B: ....

A: **Have you ever broken/injured your**.........................?
B: ....

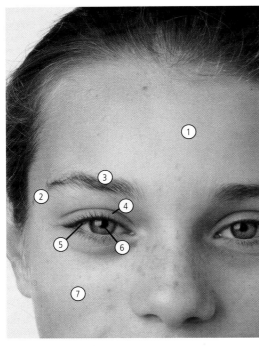

1 forehead
2 temple
3 eyebrow
4 eyelid
5 eyelash
6 pupil
7 cheek

8 tongue
9 tooth

10 brain
11 throat
12 vein
13 artery
14 lung
15 heart
16 liver
17 stomach
18 kidney
19 small intestine
20 large intestine
21 fatty tissue
22 muscles

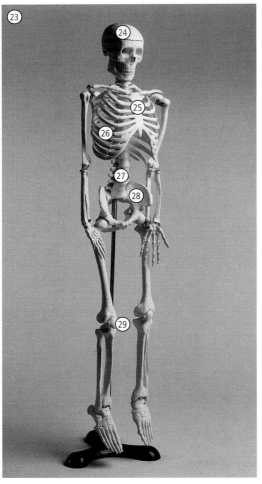

23 skeleton
24 skull
25 breastbone
26 ribs
27 spine/backbone
28 pelvis/hip-bone
29 kneecap

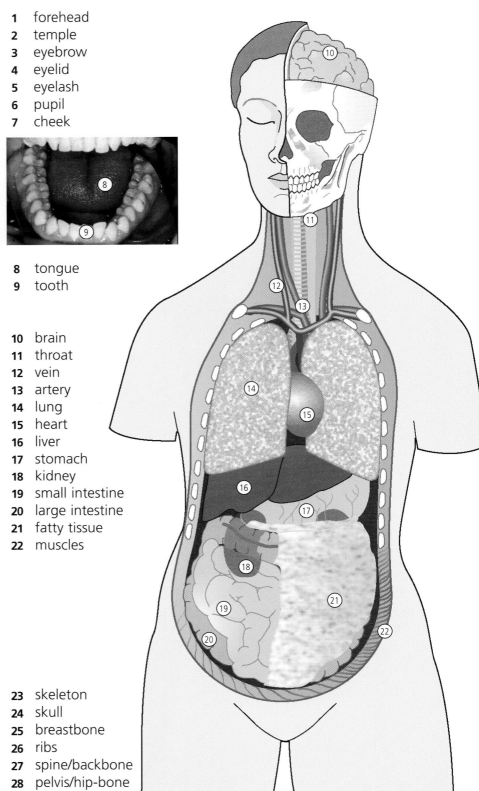

1 black hair
2 blond/fair hair
3 red/ginger hair
4 brown/dark hair
5 long hair
6 short hair
7 shoulder-length hair
8 shaved/cropped hair
9 straight hair
10 wavy hair
11 curly hair

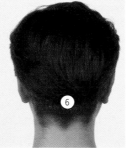
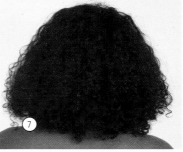
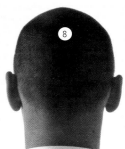

12 pony tail
13 plait
14 parting
15 fringe
16 sideburns
17 goatee
18 stubble

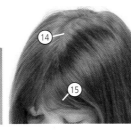
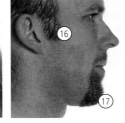
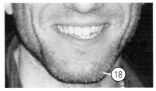

19 moustache
20 beard
21 bald
22 short
23 tall
24 slim
25 overweight

What does he look like? (25)
He's overweight and he's got short dark hair.

What does she look like? (7)
She's got curly, shoulder-length hair.

A: What does she look like? (3)
B: She ....

A: What does he/she look like?
B: He/She ....

Questions for discussion
1 What do you look like?
2 What do other members of your family look like?

1 fall
2 talk/speak
3 touch
4 stand
5 lie down
6 hug
7 wave
8 cry
9 sit
10 smile
11 laugh

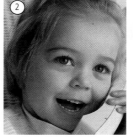

12 carry
13 frown
14 dance
15 sing
16 point
17 shake hands
18 kiss
19 push
20 pull
21 clap

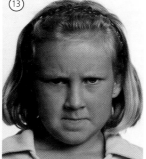

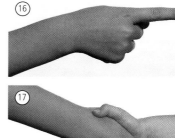

What's she doing? (7)
She's waving.

What are they doing? (6)
They're hugging.

A: **What's he/she doing?/What are they doing?**

B: He/She's ..../They're ....

Questions for discussion
1 What do you do when you're happy?
2 What do you do when you're sad?

1 read
2 pick up
3 put down
4 write
5 give
6 take

7 draw
8 cut
9 glue
10 press
11 tear
12 fold
13 paint
14 open

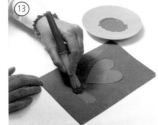

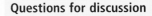

15 hold
16 fill
17 pour
18 stir
19 break

Give me that bag.

Don't open your book.

Fold the paper, but don't cut it.

A: **Take a piece of paper. Pick up your pen. Draw a tree. Don't write your name.**

Questions for discussion

Take turns to give and follow instructions.

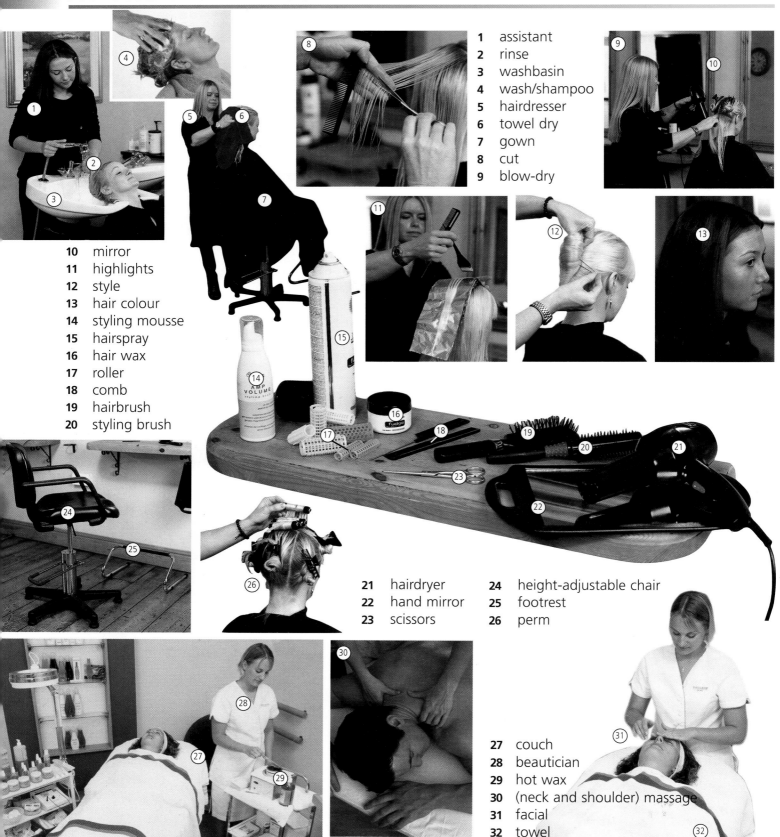

1 assistant
2 rinse
3 washbasin
4 wash/shampoo
5 hairdresser
6 towel dry
7 gown
8 cut
9 blow-dry

10 mirror
11 highlights
12 style
13 hair colour
14 styling mousse
15 hairspray
16 hair wax
17 roller
18 comb
19 hairbrush
20 styling brush

21 hairdryer
22 hand mirror
23 scissors
24 height-adjustable chair
25 footrest
26 perm

27 couch
28 beautician
29 hot wax
30 (neck and shoulder) massage
31 facial
32 towel

What's hairspray used for?
It's used for fixing hairstyles.

What are scissors used for?
They're used for cutting hair.

A: **What are rollers used for?**
B: They're used for ....

A: **What's (a) .... used for?**
B: It's used for ....

Questions for discussion
1 What does the hairdresser usually do to your hair?
2 Which of these things do you have at home?

A COSMETICS/MAKE-UP

1 eyeliner
2 eyebrow pencil
3 eye shadow
4 base/foundation
5 blusher/rouge
6 brush
7 lipstick
8 mascara
9 moisturiser

B MANICURE ITEMS

10 nail clippers
11 nail scissors
12 emery board
13 nail file
14 nail polish/varnish

C TOILETRIES

15 electric shaver
16 shaving gel
17 aftershave
18 razor
19 razor blade
20 shampoo
21 conditioner
22 perfume
23 cologne
24 tweezers
25 comb
26 hairbrush
27 hairdryer

How often do you use mascara?

I sometimes use mascara.
I never use mascara.

A: How often do you use (a) ....?
B: I never/rarely/sometimes/often/always use (a) ....

Questions for discussion

1 Which of these things are commonly used by both men and women?
2 Which of these things usually smell nice?

5.1 MINOR AILMENTS

1 she's got toothache
2 she's got stomachache
3 he's got a headache
4 he's got flu/a cold
5 he's got a sore throat
6 he's got a cough
7 he's hurt his hand
8 he's got backache
9 she's got a temperature
10 he's broken his leg
11 she's got a nose bleed
12 she's fallen over
13 he's sprained his ankle

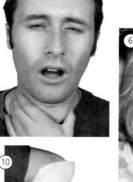

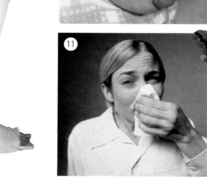

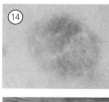
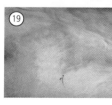

14 bruise
15 sunburn
16 scratch
17 cut
18 graze
19 scar
20 insect bite
21 rash
22 black eye
23 blood

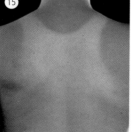
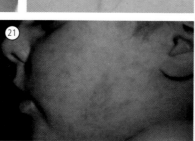
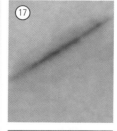

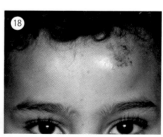

What's the matter with her? (9)
She's got a temperature.

What's wrong with him? (13)
He's sprained his ankle.

A: **What's the matter/
What's wrong with him/her?**
B: He/She's ....

Questions for discussion
1 Is anything wrong with you at the moment?
2 When was the last time you were ill? What was the matter?

For irritated eyes
1 eye drops

For a cough
2 throat lozenges
3 cough mixture

For an insect bite
4 cream
5 insect repellent

For hayfever/allergy
6 antihistamine tablets

For a cold
7 cold remedy
8 tissues

For cracked lips
9 lip balm

For a temperature
10 thermometer

For a headache
11 painkiller

For stomachache
12 antacid/Alka Seltzer™

For a cut
13 (sticking) plaster

For a graze
14 gauze (pad)
15 plasters

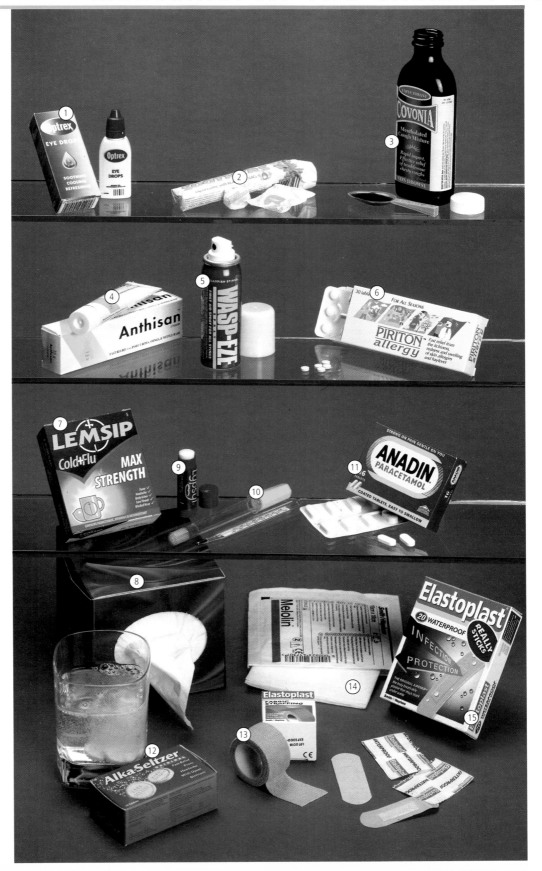

I've got stomachache.
You should take some antacid.

I've got an insect bite.
You should use some cream.

A: **I've got hayfever.**
B: You should take ....

A: **I've got (a/an)** ....
B: You should take/use some/a/an ....

Questions for discussion
1 Which of these things do you have at home?
2 Which of these things would you take on holiday with you?

MEDICAL CARE

THE DOCTOR'S SURGERY

1 doctor/general practitioner (GP)
2 X-ray
3 examination couch
4 patient
5 height chart
6 scales
7 nurse
8 medical records
9 blood pressure gauge
10 prescription
11 stethoscope

Metres
3
2.5
2
1.5

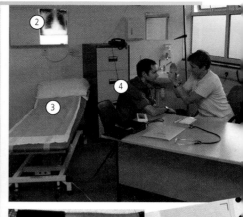
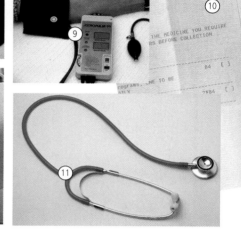

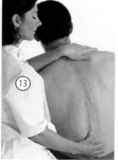

MEDICAL SPECIALISTS

12 cardiologist
13 osteopath
14 ear, nose, throat specialist
15 paediatrician
16 physiotherapist
17 obstetrician/gynaecologist
18 ophthalmologist
19 chiropodist
20 counsellor/therapist
21 dietician
22 dermatologist

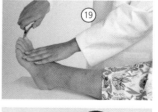
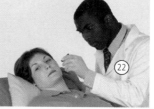

What's a dermatologist?

A dermatologist is a doctor who deals with the skin.

A: What's a/an ....?
B: A .... is a ....
who/that ....

Questions for discussion

1 Is your doctor's surgery like the ones in the photos?
2 Have you ever visited any of these specialists?

A HOSPITAL WARD

1 nurse
2 consultant
3 patient
4 waiting room
5 (hospital) trolley
6 (hospital) porter
7 X-rays
8 injection
9 needle
10 syringe
11 scanner
12 stitches
13 crutch
14 plaster cast
15 sling
16 surgical collar
17 wheelchair
18 medical chart

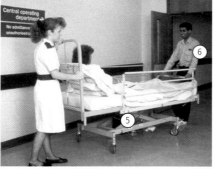

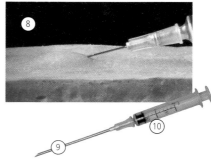
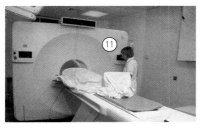

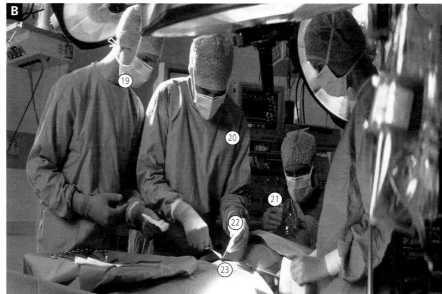
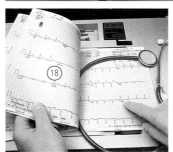
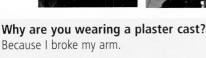

B OPERATING THEATRE

19 mask
20 surgeon
21 anaesthetist
22 surgical glove
23 operation
24 scalpel

Why are you wearing a plaster cast?
Because I broke my arm.

Why did they give you a surgical collar?
Because I hurt my neck.

A: Why are you wearing/using
..............................?/Why did they give
you ....?
B: Because ....

Questions for discussion
Describe what happens if you go
to hospital with:
1 a broken leg
2 a bad cut on your arm

1 dentist
2 dental nurse
3 patient
4 lamp
5 (oral) hygienist
6 basin
7 drill
8 dentures
9 orthodontist
10 mouthwash
11 dental floss
12 toothpaste
13 toothbrush
14 toothpick
15 mirror
16 decay
17 tooth
18 gum
19 plaque
20 back teeth
21 front teeth
22 filling
23 brace

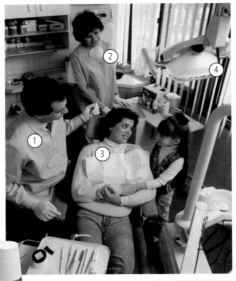
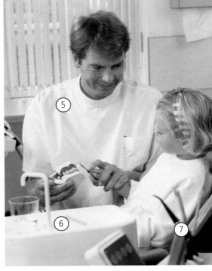

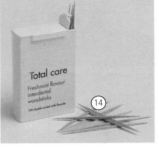

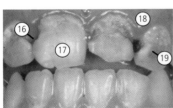
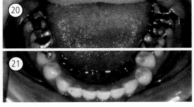
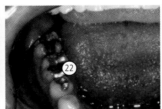
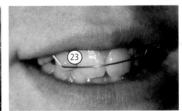

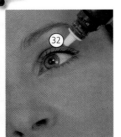
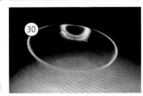

24 optician
25 alphabet board
26 glasses case
27 frame
28 lens
29 glasses
30 contact lens
31 cleaning fluid
32 eye drops

How often do you go to the dentist's?
Three times a year.

How often do you use dental floss?
Twice a week.

A: How often do you use a toothbrush?
B: Once a day.

A: How often do you ....?
B: Once/Twice/Three times a ....
/Never.

Questions for discussion
1 When did you last visit a dentist?
2 What did he/she do?
3 Do you regularly visit an optician?

OUTDOOR CLOTHING
1 rain hat
2 coat
3 raincoat
4 umbrella
5 hat
6 jacket
7 gloves
8 fleece

SWEATERS
9 crewneck jumper/sweater
10 poloneck jumper/sweater
11 V-neck jumper/sweater
12 hooded top
13 cardigan

FOOTWEAR
14 walking boots
15 boots
16 sandals
17 shoes
18 slippers
19 court shoes, pumps *AmE*

NIGHTCLOTHES
20 nightdress/nightie
21 dressing gown
22 pyjamas
23 bathrobe

Do you prefer coats or jackets?
I prefer jackets.

Do you prefer sandals or boots?
I prefer sandals.

A: Do you prefer ....
or ....?
B: I prefer ....

Questions for discussion
1 Which of these things do you need in wet or cold weather?
2 Which of these things do you only wear in the house?

FORMAL WEAR

1 suit
2 jacket
3 blouse
4 skirt
5 dress
6 evening gown/ball gown

UNDERWEAR

7 ankle socks
8 slip
9 tights
10 bra
11 knickers, panties *AmE*
12 socks
13 stockings

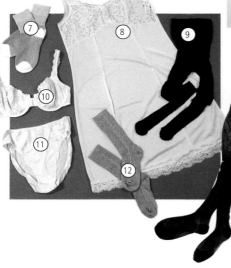

CASUAL WEAR

14 sweatshirt
15 jeans
16 trousers, pants *AmE*
17 T-shirt
18 shorts
19 top
20 leggings
21 dungarees

What colour is the evening gown?
It's red.

What colour are the tights?
They're black.

A: What colour is/are the
...........................?
B: It's/They're (light/dark)
....

Questions for discussion

1 Describe the clothes that you, or a woman that you know, usually wear(s).

2 In your opinion, which type of clothes look best on a woman?

FORMAL WEAR

1 suit
2 tie
3 jacket
4 tuxedo/dinner jacket
5 bow tie
6 waistcoat
7 shirt

CASUAL WEAR

8 jeans
9 T-shirt
10 baseball cap
11 shirt
12 trousers, pants *AmE*
13 jacket
14 sweatshirt

UNDERWEAR

15 socks
16 vest/undershirt
17 underpants
18 (boxer) shorts

SPORTSWEAR

19 tracksuit
20 bikini
21 swimming costume /swimsuit
22 swimming trunks
23 trainers

Do you like this waistcoat?
Yes, I do.

Do you like these socks?
No, I don't.

A: Do you like this shirt? (11)
B: ....

A: Do you like this/these ....?
B: Yes, I do./No, I don't.

Questions for discussion

1 Describe the clothes that you, or a man that you know, usually wear(s).
2 Which type of clothes look best on a man?

DESCRIBING CLOTHES

PARTS OF CLOTHES AND SHOES

1 lapel
2 collar
3 sleeve
4 hood
5 shoelace
6 buckle
7 heel
8 sole
9 hemline
10 button
11 buttonhole
12 pocket

13 seam
14 zip
15 cuff
16 waistband

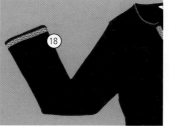

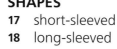

SHAPES

17 short-sleeved
18 long-sleeved
19 wide
20 narrow
21 loose
22 tight
23 baggy

Can a shirt have sleeves?
Yes, it can.

Can trousers have a hood?
No, they can't.

A: **Can (a)** .... **have** ....?
B: Yes, it/they can./No, it/they can't.

Questions for discussion

1 Do you prefer shoes with high heels or low heels?
2 Do you prefer jackets with wide or narrow lapels?
3 Do you prefer long-sleeved or short-sleeved shirts?

COLOURS

1 white
2 light blue
3 yellow
4 navy blue
5 camel
6 pink
7 brown
8 green
9 purple
10 beige
11 cream
12 blue
13 red
14 grey
15 orange
16 black
17 turquoise

PATTERNS

18 striped
19 spotted
20 patterned
21 plain
22 tartan
23 checked

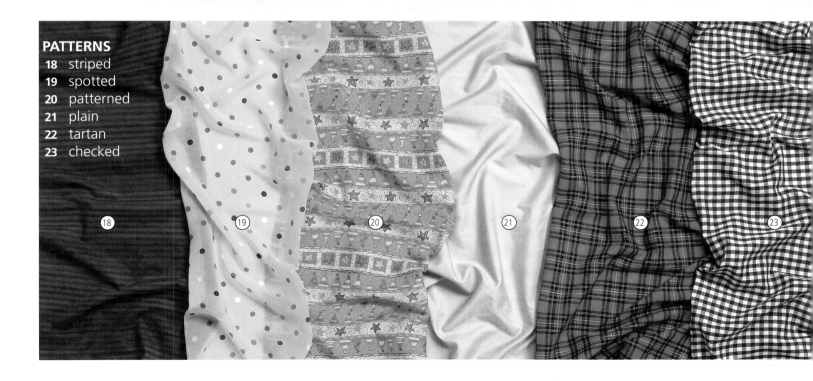

Which colours do you like?
Yellow and red.

Which fabric do you like?
The tartan one.

A: Which .... do you like?
B: The .... one (and the
.... one).

Questions for discussion

1 Which of these colours and patterns do you often wear?
2 Describe what the person next to you is wearing.

FABRICS, SEWING AND KNITTING

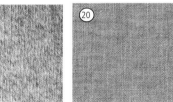
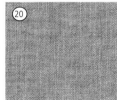

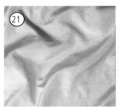
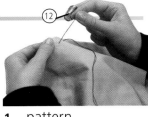

1 pattern
2 iron-on tape
3 Velcro™
4 scissors
5 needle
6 thread
7 sewing basket
8 tape measure
9 pin cushion
10 wool
11 knitting needle
12 thimble
13 hook and eye
14 press stud (popper)

15 polyester
16 denim
17 cotton
18 leather
19 wool
20 linen
21 silk

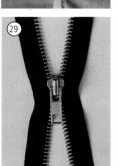

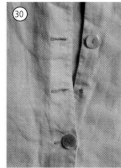

22 sewing machine
23 safety pin
24 pin
25 dressmaker
26 tailor
27 rip/tear
28 stain
29 broken zip
30 missing button

What is Velcro used for?
It's used to join two pieces of fabric together.

What are scissors used for?
They're used to cut fabric.

A: What is/are (a)
.... **used for?**
B: It's/They're used to
....

Questions for discussion
1 Which of the things do you have at home?
2 What should you do for each of the problems (27–30)?

A JEWELLERY

1 money clip
2 cuff link
3 tie clip
4 watch
5 handkerchief
6 chain
7 brooch
8 necklaces
9 earring
10 pearls
11 ring
12 hair slide
13 bracelet

B METALS

14 gold
15 silver

C GEMS

16 diamond
17 emerald
18 ruby
19 amethyst
20 sapphire
21 topaz

D ACCESSORIES

22 braces, suspenders *AmE*
23 shoulder bag
24 document case
25 Filofax™/personal organiser
26 make-up bag
27 shopping bag
28 handbag
29 clutch bag
30 key ring
31 scarf
32 briefcase
33 wallet
34 purse
35 belt
36 buckle

That's a nice belt.
I agree./I disagree. I don't like it.

Those are nice earrings.
I agree./I disagree. I don't like them.

A: That's a nice/Those are nice
....
B: I agree/disagree. I don't like it/them.

Questions for discussion
In your opinion, which of these things:
1 are expensive?
2 are useful?

1 nursery school/pre-school
2 primary school

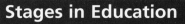

Stages in Education

Foundation:	ages 3 to end of reception nursery or pre-school	
Primary (children aged 5 to 11)		
Key Stage 1	Year 1 5–6 years old Year 2 6–7 years old	
Key Stage 2	Year 3 7–8 years old Year 4 8–9 years old Year 5 9–10 years old Year 6 10–11 years old	
Secondary (students aged 11 to 18)		**Qualifications**
Key Stage 3	Year 7 11–12 years old Year 8 12–13 years old Year 9 13–14 years old	
Key Stage 4	Year 10 14–15 years old Year 11 15–16 years old	GCSE (General Certificate of Secondary Education), GNVQ (General National Vocational Qualification)
Key Stage 5	(non compulsory) Year 12 16–17 years old Year 13 17–18 years old	AS-level (Advanced Subsidiary), A-level (Advanced Level)

3 secondary school
4 boarding school
5 dormitory
6 A-level student

7 university
8 university graduates

University Qualifications

Undergraduate qualifications (after 2–4 years)	HND	Higher National Diploma
	Dip HE	Diploma of Higher Education
	BA	Bachelor of Arts
	BSc	Bachelor of Science
	BEd	Bachelor of Education
Postgraduate qualifications (2 years + after the first degree)	PGCE	Postgraduate Certificate of Education
	MA	Master of Arts
	MSc	Master of Science
	MEd	Master of Education
	MBA	Master of Business Administration
	M Phil	Master of Philosophy
	PhD	Doctor of Philosophy

the tables show a simplified structure and only the main qualifications

1 kite
2 swings
3 slide
4 roundabout
5 scooter
6 tricycle
7 doll's pram
8 bench
9 sandpit
10 sand
11 climbing frame
12 seesaw
13 skateboard
14 roller skates
15 doll

16 pre-school
17 toy
18 colouring book
19 book
20 crayons
21 paintbrush
22 paintbox
23 rounded scissors
24 glue
25 building blocks/bricks
26 jigsaw puzzle
27 easel

What colour is the tricycle? (6)
It's red and yellow.

What colour are the roller skates? (14)
They're pink and purple.

A: **What colour is/are the**
   ....?
B: It's/They're ....

Questions for discussion

1 Which of these things have wheels?

2 Did you have any of these things when you were little?

51

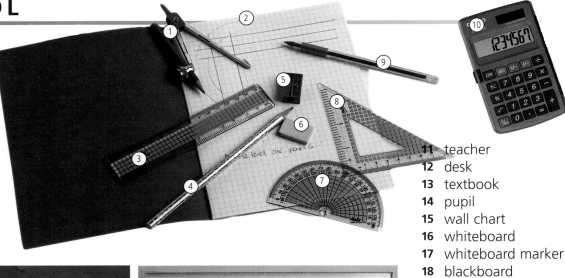

THE CLASSROOM

1 compass
2 exercise book
3 ruler
4 pencil
5 pencil sharpener
6 rubber
7 protractor
8 set square
9 (ballpoint) pen/biro™
10 calculator

11 teacher
12 desk
13 textbook
14 pupil
15 wall chart
16 whiteboard
17 whiteboard marker
18 blackboard
19 chalk

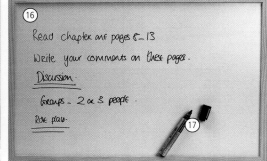

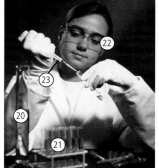

THE SCIENCE LAB

20 measuring cylinder
21 test tubes
22 safety glasses
23 pipette
24 measuring beaker
25 bunsen burner
26 tongs

THE GYM

27 wall bars
28 mat
29 (pommel) horse

TECHNOLOGY IN THE CLASSROOM

30 CD player
31 video recorder
32 computer
33 language lab booth
34 overhead projector

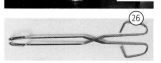
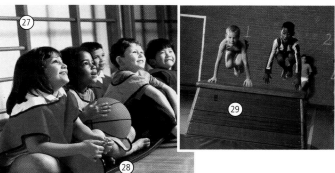

PRIMARY SCHOOL AND SECONDARY SCHOOL

1 maths
2 science
3 music
4 PE (physical education)
5 history
6 English
7 RE (religious education)
8 art
9 geography
10 IT (information technology)

RELIGIONS
Alan Brown
John Rankin
Angela Wood

LONGMAN STUDY GUIDES GCSE KEY STAGE 4
World History

JANE AUSTEN
...sten was born in 1775. As a teenager, Jane started writing plays and books. However, writing novels was not considered the profession of a lady, so in 1811 she published her first novel, *Sense and Sensibility*, anonymously. She wrote five more novels, including *Pride and Prejudice* and *Persuasion* before she died in 1817.

SECONDARY SCHOOL ONLY

11 chemistry
12 physics
13 design and technology
14 biology
15 performing arts (drama)
16 sociology
17 business studies
18 Latin
19 Spanish
20 French
21 German

THE LATIN LANGUAGE
Prepared by the Scottish Classics Group

français *direct*
Richard Marsden
Anne Ryan
David Forth
LONGMAN

LONGMAN STUDY GUIDES GCSE KEY STAGE 4
Spanish

Ja!

Do you like geography at school?
No, I don't.

Did you like maths at school?
Yes, I did.

A: Do/Did you enjoy .... at school?
B: Yes, I do./No, I don't./Yes, I did./No, I didn't.

Questions for discussion
What subjects do schoolchildren study in your country?

A TUTORIAL
1 lecturer's/tutor's office
2 tutor

B CAMPUS
3 student welfare office
4 cafeteria

C LECTURE
5 lecture hall
6 lecturer

D LIBRARY
7 reference section
8 information desk
9 lending desk
10 checkout desk
11 librarian
12 encyclopedia
13 dictionary

14 atlas
15 library card
16 periodical section
17 journal
18 microfiche
19 microfiche reader
20 shelves
21 information section
22 library assistant
23 photocopier

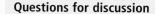

What's an atlas?
It's a book that contains maps.

What's a lecture hall?
It's a room where students listen to lectures.

A: **What's a cafeteria?**
B: ....

A: **What's a/an** ....?
B: It's a/an .... that/where/who ....

Questions for discussion
What must you do in a library if you want to:
1 take out a book?
2 look for some information?

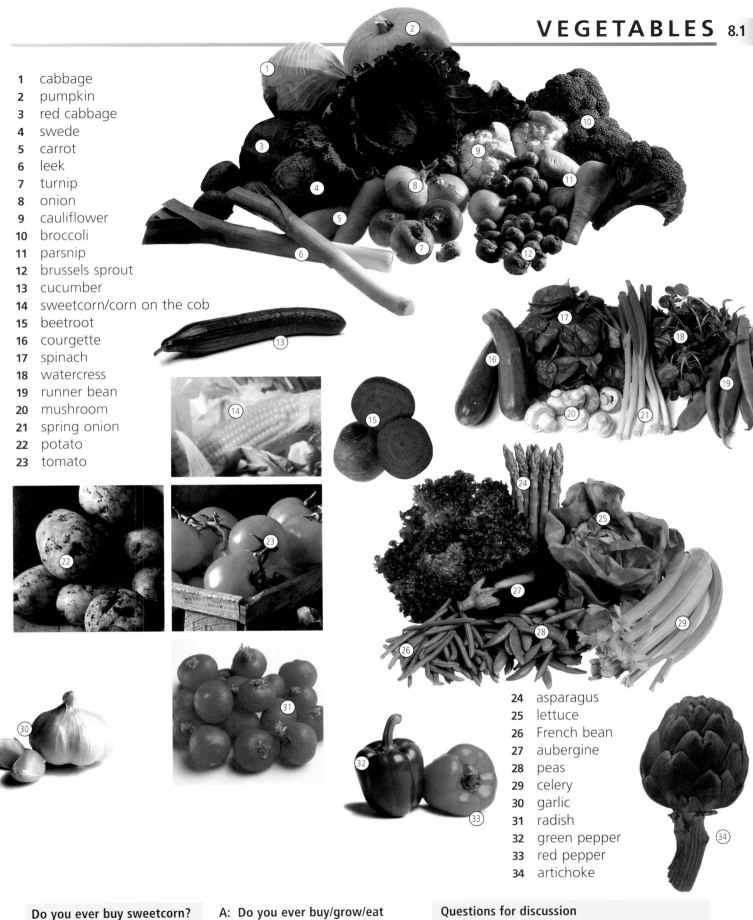

1 cabbage
2 pumpkin
3 red cabbage
4 swede
5 carrot
6 leek
7 turnip
8 onion
9 cauliflower
10 broccoli
11 parsnip
12 brussels sprout
13 cucumber
14 sweetcorn/corn on the cob
15 beetroot
16 courgette
17 spinach
18 watercress
19 runner bean
20 mushroom
21 spring onion
22 potato
23 tomato

24 asparagus
25 lettuce
26 French bean
27 aubergine
28 peas
29 celery
30 garlic
31 radish
32 green pepper
33 red pepper
34 artichoke

Do you ever buy sweetcorn?
Yes, I do.

Do you ever grow carrots?
No, I don't.

A: **Do you ever buy/grow/eat**
.... ?
B: Yes, I do./No, I don't.

Questions for discussion

1 Which of these vegetables are common in your country?
2 Which can you eat without cooking?

1 grapefruit
2 satsuma
3 clementine
4 lemon
5 lime
6 orange
7 tangerine

8 blackcurrant
9 cherry
10 starfruit
11 papaya
12 pineapple
13 mango
14 melon

15 gooseberry
16 blueberry
17 lychee
18 grape
19 avocado
20 kiwi fruit
21 banana

22 pear
23 apple
24 plum
25 strawberry
26 peach
27 raspberry
28 rhubarb
29 nectarine
30 watermelon
31 apricot

32 hazelnut
33 walnut
34 Brazil nut
35 coconut
36 cashew nut
37 peanut

38 raisin
39 fig
40 prune
41 date

Do you prefer apples or pears?
I prefer pears.

Do you prefer peaches or plums.
I don't like either.

A: **Do you prefer** .... **or**
......................?
B: I prefer ..../I don't like either.

Questions for discussion
1 Which of these fruits are common in your country?
2 Which are summer fruits?

CHECK-OUT AREA

1 cashier
2 customer/shopper
3 aisle
4 carrier bag/
    shopping bag
5 trolley
6 conveyor belt
7 shopping
8 checkout desk

FROZEN FOODS

9 pizza
10 chips
11 ice cream
12 fish fingers
13 peas
14 burgers

DAIRY PRODUCTS

15 milk
16 cream
17 cheese
18 butter
19 eggs
20 yoghurt, yogurt
21 margarine

TINNED/BOTTLED FOOD

22 sweetcorn
23 baked beans
24 corned beef
25 soup
26 tuna
27 honey
28 chopped tomatoes
29 jam

DRY GOODS

1 pasta
2 rice
3 coffee
4 cocoa
5 herbal tea
6 biscuits
7 oats
8 tea
9 flour
10 cereal

CONDIMENTS

11 mayonnaise
12 sugar
13 ketchup
14 vinegar
15 mustard
16 salad dressing
17 herbs and spices
18 oil
19 salt
20 pepper

DRINKS

21 white wine
22 beer
23 red wine
24 lemonade
25 orange juice
26 cola
27 mineral water

HOUSEHOLD PRODUCTS

28 bin bags
29 dog food
30 cat food
31 washing powder

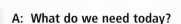

What do we need today?
We need some fish fingers and some bin bags, but we don't need any flour.

A: What do we need today?
B: We need ...., but we don't need ....

B: We need some ...., but we don't need any ....

Questions for discussion
What would you buy to make:
1 breakfast?
2 a quick dinner?

MEAT

1 sausage
2 minced beef
3 chicken leg
4 bacon
5 turkey
6 leg of lamb
7 beef joint
8 pork chops
9 lamb chops
10 steak
11 liver
12 stewing beef

DELICATESSEN

13 blue cheese
14 Swiss cheese
15 brie
16 coleslaw
17 hummus
18 taramasalata
19 smoked ham
20 ham
21 pie

FISH AND SEAFOOD

22 whole trout
23 salmon steaks
24 cod fillet
25 prawns
26 lobster
27 crab
28 mussels

BAKERY

29 wholemeal bread
30 bagel
31 cake
32 white bread
33 pitta bread
34 baguette
35 naan bread

1 waiter
2 menu
3 wine list
4 dessert trolley

Wine List

White	Per bottle
Australian Chardonnay	£10.99
New Zealand Sauvignon Blanc	£8.99
House White	£6.99
Red	
Australian Shiraz	£10.99
Cotes Du Rhone	£8.99
House Red	£6.99
House Champagne	£22.99

STARTERS/HORS D'ŒUVRES

5 tomato soup
6 melon
7 chicken liver pâté
8 prawn cocktail
9 smoked salmon

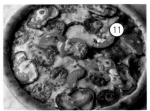

MAIN COURSES

10 stuffed peppers
11 pizza
12 lasagne
13 roast beef with Yorkshire pudding
14 sole with butter sauce

SIDE VEGETABLES

15 roast potatoes
16 mixed vegetables
17 carrots
18 side salad

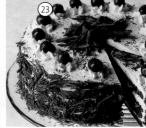

DRINKS

24 coffee
25 tea
26 milk
27 fizzy mineral water
28 still mineral water
29 white wine
30 champagne
31 red wine

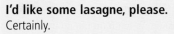

DESSERTS

19 cream
20 ice cream
21 cheesecake
22 apple pie
23 (chocolate) gateau

I'd like some lasagne, please.
Certainly.

I'd like some roast potatoes, please.
I'm sorry, we haven't got any today.

A: **I'd like some ...., please.**
B: Certainly./I'm sorry, we haven't got any today.

Questions for discussion

1 Which of these foods are common in your country?
2 What would you like for dinner?

1 mustard
2 tomato ketchup
3 sachet of pepper
4 sachet of salt
5 (paper) napkin
6 cola
7 cheeseburger
8 beefburger/hamburger
9 straw
10 milk shake
11 fizzy drink
12 hot dog
13 chips/French fries
14 cone
15 ice cream

16 gherkins
17 peanuts
18 crisps, chips *AmE*
19 nuts and raisins

20 doughnut
21 muffin
22 fish and chips
23 vinegar
24 fried chicken
25 sweets, candy *AmE*
26 ploughman's lunch

Would you like a hamburger?
Yes, please.

Would you like some peanuts?
No, thanks.

A: **Would you like some ketchup?**
B: ....

A: **Would you like a/some** ....?
B: Yes, please./No, thanks.

Questions for discussion
1 Which of these things are sweet?
2 Do you dislike any of these things?
3 How often do you buy fast food?

CONTAINERS AND QUANTITIES

1 bottle
2 tin
3 packet
4 jar
5 tub/container
6 box
7 carton
8 bag
9 can
10 six-pack
11 roll
12 loaf

13 tube
14 a cupful
15 a teaspoonful
16 a tablespoonful

17 1 metre
18 1 centimetre
19 1 millimetre

20 empty
21 one quarter/a quarter
22 one third/a third
23 one half/a half
24 three quarters
25 full

26 100 grams
27 1 kilogram
28 100 millilitres
29 1 litre

How much milk do we want?
Four litres./Two cartons.

How many bottles of cola do we want?
Two.

A: **How much .... do we want?/How many .... of .... do we want?**
B: ....

Questions for discussion
Which of these containers can be made of:
1 paper? 2 plastic?
3 glass? 4 metal?

1 cook
2 wash (salad)
3 peel (potatoes)
4 grate (cheese)
5 chop
6 crush (garlic)
7 beat (eggs)
8 cut up
9 rub in (flour and butter)
10 slice
11 grease (a tin)
12 break (an egg)
13 stir
14 mix (ingredients)
15 knead (dough)
16 steam
17 sauté
18 boil (eggs)
19 add (liquid)
20 bake
21 pour (water)
22 weigh (beans)
23 stir fry
24 grill
25 roast
26 barbecue
27 measure ingredients
28 fry (an egg)

What's he doing? (6)
He's crushing garlic.

What's he doing? (18)
He's boiling an egg.

A: **What's he doing?** (11)
B: He's ....

A: **What's he doing?**
B: He's ....

Questions for discussion

1 In what different ways can you cook meat?

2 Explain how you make one of your favourite dishes.

BREAKFAST

1 porridge
2 cereal
3 bread
4 full cream milk
5 semi-skimmed milk
6 muesli
7 grapefruit
8 tea
9 coffee
10 boiled egg
11 butter
12 toast
13 croissant
14 jam
15 marmalade

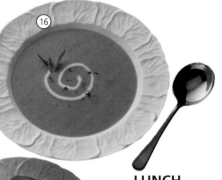

LUNCH

16 soup and bread roll
17 cheese on toast
18 ham salad
19 sandwiches

DINNER

20 spaghetti bolognese
21 shepherd's pie with vegetables
22 chicken curry with rice
23 fish fingers with mashed potatoes
24 omelette

Would you like some toast?
No, thanks. I'd rather have a croissant.

Would you like some muesli?
Yes, please.

A: **Would you like a/some** ....?
B: No, thanks. I'd rather have a/some
   ..../Yes, please.

Questions for discussion
What things do you usually eat for:
1 breakfast?
2 lunch?

1 railway station
2 clock
3 arrivals and departures board
4 platform entrance
5 passenger
6 train
7 engine
8 carriage
9 track
10 the underground
11 platform
12 (return) ticket
13 second class
14 first class
15 rush hour

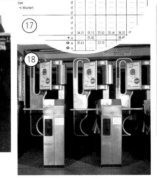

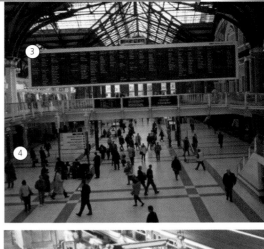

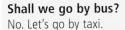

20 minicab
21 taxi
22 (taxi) driver
23 black cab

16 kiosk
17 timetable
18 barrier
19 tunnel

24 luggage compartment
25 coach
26 (bus) driver
27 bus
28 bus stop

Shall we go by bus?
No. Let's go by taxi.

Shall we go by underground?
No. Let's go by bus.

A: **Shall we go by minicab?**
B: No. Let's ....

A: **Shall we go by ....?**
B: No. Let's go by ....

Questions for discussion
1 Where is the nearest train station to your house?
2 Which forms of public transport do you use?

A CARS

1 hatchback
2 saloon car
3 estate car
4 people carrier
5 four-wheel drive
6 convertible
7 sports car

B TWO-WHEELED VEHICLES

8 motor scooter
9 bicycle
10 motorbike

C OTHER VEHICLES

11 van
12 caravan
13 minibus
14 lorry, truck *AmE*
15 tractor
16 articulated lorry

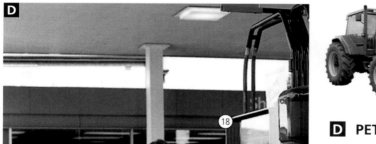

D PETROL STATION/GARAGE

17 nozzle
18 petrol pump
19 hose

E ENGINE

20 distributor
21 cylinder block
22 air filter
23 battery

1 rear windscreen
2 rearview mirror
3 brake light
4 boot
5 numberplate
6 bumper
7 exhaust pipe
8 headrest
9 seat belt
10 roof-rack
11 door
12 windscreen wiper
13 wing mirror
14 bonnet
15 headlight
16 indicator
17 sidelight
18 soft top
19 petrol cap
20 wing
21 wheel
22 tyre

23 ignition
24 dashboard
25 clutch
26 brake
27 accelerator
28 steering wheel
29 temperature gauge
30 rev counter
31 speedometer
32 fuel gauge
33 radio/cassette/CD player
34 gear lever/stick, gear shift *AmE*
35 electric window button

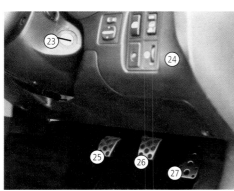

What's the matter with the car?
The speedometer is broken.

What's wrong with the car?
The headlights don't work.

A: **What's the matter/What's wrong with the car?**
B: The .... is/are broken./The .... doesn't/don't work.

Questions for discussion

1 Do you have any of these vehicles?
2 Which of these things need electricity?
3 What repairs has your vehicle had recently?

A MOTORWAY
1 flyover
2 hard shoulder
3 inside lane
4 middle lane
5 outside lane
6 bridge

B DUAL CARRIAGEWAY
7 central reservation
8 slip road
9 cat's eyes

C JUNCTION
10 streetlight/lamp-post
11 crossroads
12 traffic lights
13 red
14 amber
15 green

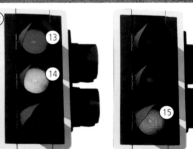

16 lorry
17 zebra crossing
18 pedestrian
19 (pedestrian) underpass

D ROUNDABOUT
20 bus
21 car

You mustn't park on the hard shoulder if you are on a motorway.

You must wait at a roundabout if a vehicle is going round it.

A: You .... if the traffic lights are red.

A: You must/mustn't .... if ....

Questions for discussion
Discuss other things you must and mustn't do if you are driving.

E LEVEL CROSSING

22 barrier
23 railway track

F ROADWORKS

24 traffic cone

G SIGNS

25 give way sign
26 stop sign
27 roadsign
28 no right turn sign
29 no U-turn sign
30 no overtaking sign
31 steep hill sign
32 no through road sign
33 cyclists only sign
34 slippery road sign
35 roadworks ahead sign
36 roundabout sign
37 level crossing sign

A: **What does this sign mean? (30)**
B: It means that you mustn't overtake.

A: **What does this sign mean? (37)**
B: It means that there's a level crossing.

A: **What does this sign mean?**
B: It means that you must/mustn't ....
/It means that there's a/there are ....

Questions for discussion
How are roads and roadsigns different in your country?

THE TERMINAL

1 check-in desk
2 ticket
3 departure gates
4 metal detector
5 luggage/baggage
6 porter
7 luggage trolley
8 suitcase
9 flight information screens
10 security
11 X-ray scanner
12 hand luggage
13 duty-free shop
14 passport control
15 passport
16 immigration officer

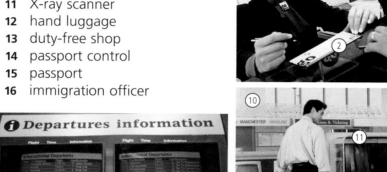

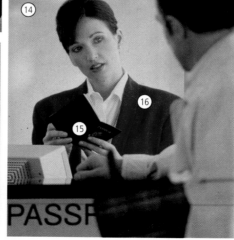

17 baggage reclaim area
18 baggage carousel
19 boarding pass
20 customs
21 customs officer

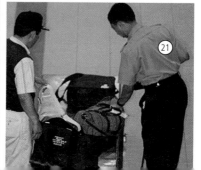

A ON BOARD

1 window
2 window seat
3 aisle seat
4 flight attendant
5 tray
6 armrest
7 cockpit
8 pilot/captain
9 instrument panel
10 co-pilot
11 oxygen mask
12 cabin
13 overhead (luggage) compartment
14 jet engine
15 life jacket

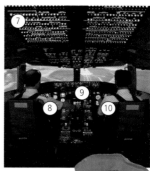

ADULT/CHILD
RFD LIFEJACKET

B THE RUNWAY

16 take-off
17 runway
18 wing
19 trailer
20 landing
21 tail
22 jet (plane)
23 rotor
24 helicopter
25 control tower
26 air traffic controller
27 hangar

Where's the pilot?
He's in the cockpit.

Where's the plane?
It's on the runway.

A: **Where's the tray?**
B: It's ....

A: **Where's the** ....?
B: It's/He's/She's in/on the ....

Questions for discussion
1 What happens in a departure hall?
2 What happens in a duty free shop?
3 What happens in a customs area?

1 life jacket
2 lifeboat
3 liner/cruise ship
4 (oil) tanker
5 ferry

6 sailing ship
7 sail
8 mast
9 cable
10 anchor
11 lighthouse

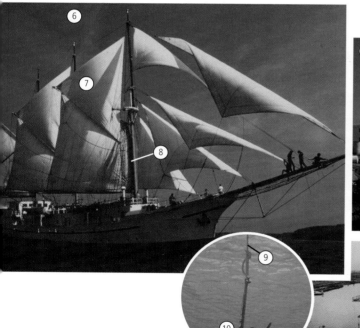

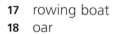

12 marina
13 motor boat
14 yacht, sailboat *AmE*
15 cabin cruiser
16 cabin

17 rowing boat
18 oar

19 crane
20 ship
21 dock
22 cargo

23 bow
24 stern
25 deck

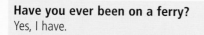

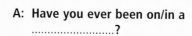

Have you ever been on a ferry?
Yes, I have.

Have you ever been in a yacht?
No, I haven't.

A: **Have you ever been on/in a**
.........................?
B: Yes, I have./No, I haven't.

Questions for discussion
Which of these boats do you think is:
1 the slowest/fastest?
2 the heaviest?

1 customer
2 cashier/bank clerk
3 counter

4 cashpoint
5 cashpoint card/debit card
6 pin number
7 deposit box/slot
8 exchange rates
9 financial adviser
10 online banking

11 paying-in slip
12 credit card
13 bank statement
14 bank account number
15 bank balance
16 withdrawal slip
17 stub
18 cheque card
19 cheque
20 chequebook

1 one
3 three
5 five
9 nine

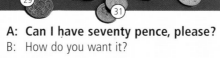
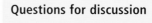

21 cash
22 fifty pounds/fifty pound note
23 twenty pounds/twenty pound note
24 ten pounds/ten pound note
25 five pounds/five pound note
26 two pounds/two pound coin
27 one pound/one pound coin
28 fifty pence/fifty pence piece
29 twenty pence/twenty pence piece
30 ten pence/ten pence piece
31 five pence/five pence piece
32 two pence/two pence piece
33 one penny/one penny piece

34 traveller's cheque
35 foreign currency

Can I have thirty pounds, please?
How do you want it?

Three ten pound notes, please.
Here you are.

A: **Can I have seventy pence, please?**
B: How do you want it?

A: ...., please.
B: ....

Questions for discussion
1 What different notes and coins are there in your country?
2 How often do you pay by cheque?

1 CCTV camera
2 roadsign
3 Belisha beacon
4 zebra crossing
5 department store
6 bus
7 street
8 railings
9 offices
10 traffic
11 parking notice
12 bus shelter
13 bus stop
14 bollard
15 parking meter

16 bus lane
17 double yellow line
18 pedestrian
19 pavement
20 gutter
21 kerb
22 traffic lights

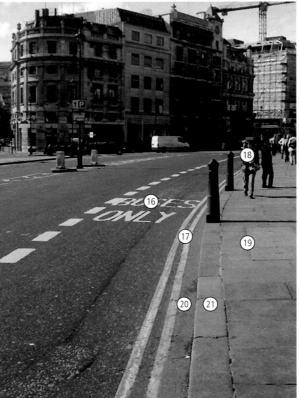

1 skyscraper
2 tower block
3 underground entrance
4 streetlight
5 newspaper vendor
6 newspaper stand
7 manhole cover
8 phone box
9 shop
10 flag
11 skyline
12 sky
13 river
14 bridge
15 (litter) bin
16 hoarding/billboard

Is there a department store in your town?
No, there isn't.

Are there any phone boxes in your town?
Yes, there are.

A: **Is there a/Are there any .... in your town?**
B: Yes, there is./No, there isn't./Yes, there are./No, there aren't.

Questions for discussion
1 Which of these things do you find in cities in your country?
2 Which of these things are for people on foot?

1 first class post
2 second class post
3 envelope
4 postmark
5 stamp
6 airmail letter
7 postcard
8 postal order
9 letter
10 (birthday) card
11 delivery
12 postman/postwoman
13 (post office) clerk
14 scales
15 counter
16 address
17 postcode
18 collection
19 pillar box
20 postbag
21 stamp machine
22 Post Office van
23 postbox/letterbox

24 Swiftair™
25 Recorded Delivery
26 Special Delivery
27 scissors
28 string
29 parcel, package *AmE*

What's that? (19)
It's a pillar box.

What are those? (2,5)
They're stamps.

A: What's that?/What are those?
B: It's a/an ..../They're
....

Questions for discussion
Imagine you are in Britain. How would you send these things:
1 a cheque to someone in your country
2 a letter to the USA

STATIONERY

1 correction fluid/Tipp-Ex™ *BrE*
2 string
3 sticky tape/Sellotape™
4 rubber
5 drawing pins
6 coloured pen
7 pencil
8 biro™
9 tube of glue
10 writing paper
11 packet of envelopes

PERIODICALS, BOOKS, ETC

12 matches
13 colour film
14 wrapping paper
15 street map
16 newspaper
17 colouring book
18 magazine
19 paperback

CONFECTIONERY

20 bag of sweets
21 packet of crisps
22 bar of chocolate
23 mints
24 chewing gum
25 lollipop
26 fudge
27 box of chocolates

Can I have one of those lollipops, please?
Here you are.

Can I have some of those mints, please?
Here you are.

A: **Can I have one of those/some of that/those ...., please?**
B: Here you are.

Questions for discussion

1 Do you buy any newspapers or magazines every week?
2 Do you buy any sweets every week?

1 music shop
2 video shop
3 chemist's
4 optician's
5 sports shop
6 sweet shop
7 toy shop
8 department store

9 book shop
10 stationer's
11 escalator
12 shoe shop
13 fabric shop
14 electronics shop
15 travel agency

I need a new TV.
Let's go to the electronics shop.

I'd like some chocolate.
Let's go to the sweet shop.

A: **I need some tennis balls.**
B: Let's ....

A: **I need/'d like a/an/some ... .**
B: Let's go to the ....

Questions for discussion

Which of these shops:
1 sell holidays?
2 can test your eyes?

POLICE

1. police station
2. police officer
3. police car

FIRE BRIGADE

4. fire
5. fire fighter
6. water
7. hose
8. fire engine
9. ladder
10. smoke
11. fire extinguisher

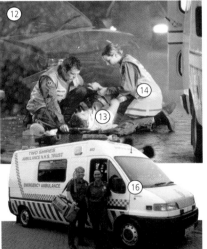

AMBULANCE SERVICE

12. road accident
13. injured person
14. paramedic
15. drip
16. ambulance
17. oxygen mask
18. stretcher

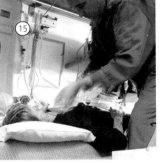

ROADSIDE BREAKDOWN

19. tow truck
20. roadside assistant

CALLING FROM A PUBLIC PHONE BOX

21. (tele)phone box
22. receiver
23. slot
24. number pad
25. phonecard
26. emergency number
27. dialling code
28. international code
29. country code

Phonecard plus

In an emergency call 999

INTERNATIONAL CODES

HOLLAND
Please see Netherlands

ICELAND
00 354
Then customer's
7 digit number

HONDURAS
00 504

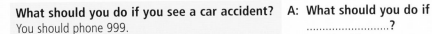

What should you do if you see a car accident?
You should phone 999.

What should you do if you see a crime?
You should tell a police officer.

A: **What should you do if ....?**

B: You should ....

Questions for discussion

Imagine you have just seen a road accident. You phone 999 (the emergency services). Roleplay the conversation with a partner.

A CRICKET

1 scoreboard
2 boundary
3 fielder
4 wicket keeper
5 cricket ball
6 wicket
7 batsman
8 (cricket) pitch
9 helmet
10 pads
11 bat
12 umpire
13 bails
14 stump
15 bowler

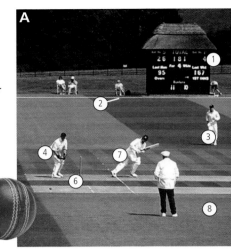

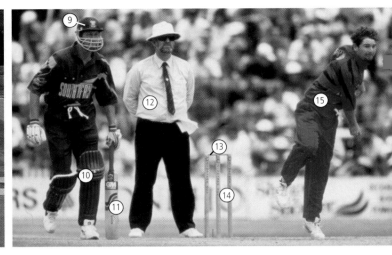

B FOOTBALL

16 stadium
17 crowd/fans
18 centre circle
19 halfway line
20 penalty box
21 penalty spot
22 goal
23 goal area
24 goal line
25 net
26 goalpost
27 football boots
28 red card
29 referee
30 player/footballer
31 goalkeeper/goalie
32 ball

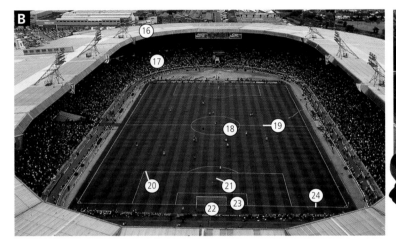

C RUGBY

33 player
34 pitch
35 posts
36 stand
37 ball

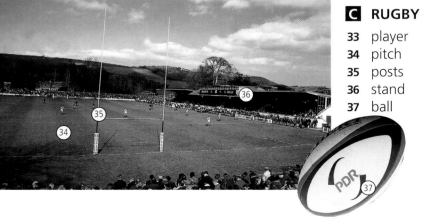

A BASKETBALL

1 backboard
2 basket
3 basketball
4 (basketball) player

B VOLLEYBALL

5 volleyball
6 net
7 (volleyball) player

C BOXING

8 glove
9 boxer
10 trunks
11 referee
12 ropes
13 ring

D HORSE RACING

14 gate
15 racehorse
16 jockey

Which is the best football team in Italy?
Juventus!

A: Which is the best .... team/ Who is the best .... in ....?
B: .... !

Questions for discussion

1 Do you do any of these sports?
2 Which of these sports is the most popular in your country?

A TENNIS
1 (tennis) racket/racquet
2 (tennis) ball
3 baseline
4 (tennis) player
5 court
6 net

B SQUASH
7 (squash) player
8 (squash) racket/racquet
9 (squash) ball

C PING PONG/TABLE TENNIS
10 (ping pong) ball
11 net
12 bat
13 (ping pong) table
14 (ping pong) player

D BADMINTON
15 shuttlecock
16 (badminton) racket/racquet
17 (badminton) player

E KARATE
18 black belt

F JUDO

G WRESTLING
19 wrestler
20 mat

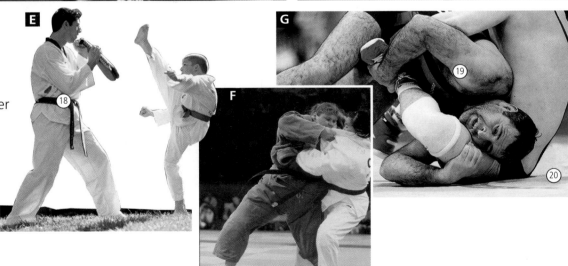

Would you like to try squash?
Yes, I would.

Would you like to try judo?
I've already tried it.

A: **Would you like to try ....?**
B: Yes, I would./No, I wouldn't./I've already tried it.

Questions for discussion
1 Which of these sports do people do indoors?
2 Which of these sports are originally from Asia?

A JOGGING
1 jogger

B RUNNING
2 runner

C CYCLING
3 helmet
4 cyclist
5 wheel
6 bicycle/bike

D HORSE RIDING
7 reins
8 horse
9 rider
10 saddle
11 stirrup

E ARCHERY
12 target
13 bow
14 arrow
15 archer

F GOLF
16 golfer
17 (golf) club
18 green
19 hole
20 (golf) ball

G HANG GLIDING
21 hang glider

H ROLLERBLADING
22 helmet
23 rollerblader
24 pads
25 in-line skate/rollerblade

I PARACHUTING/SKYDIVING
26 parachutist/sky-diver
27 parachute

J CLIMBING
28 climber
29 harness

K GYMNASTICS
30 gymnast
31 leotard
32 balance beam

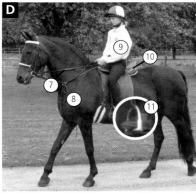
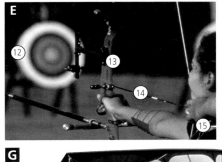

Did you go cycling last weekend?
Yes, I did.
No, I didn't.

A: Did you go ....ing/do archery/play golf last weekend?
B: Yes, I did./No, I didn't.

Questions for discussion
Which of these sports need special clothes?

WATER SPORTS

A SWIMMING
1 goggles
2 swimming hat/cap
3 swimmer
4 swimming pool

B SNORKELLING
5 snorkel
6 snorkeller

C SCUBA DIVING
7 (air) tank
8 wet suit
9 mask
10 scuba diver

D DIVING
11 diver
12 diving board

E FISHING
13 (fishing) line
14 fishing rod
15 fisherman

F SURFING AND WIND-SURFING
16 sailboard
17 wind-surfer
18 surfboard
19 surfer

G ROWING
20 oar
21 rowing boat
22 rower

H CANOEING
23 paddle
24 canoeist
25 canoe

I SAILING
26 sail
27 mast
28 sailing boat

J WATER SKIING
29 towrope
30 motorboat
31 water skier
32 water ski

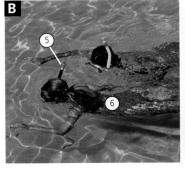

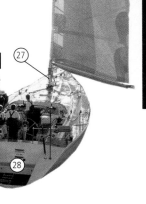

A SLEDGING
1 sledge
2 snow

B DOWNHILL SKIING
3 skier
4 pole
5 (ski) boot
6 ski
7 chairlift
8 snowboard

C SPEED SKATING
9 speed skater
10 skate
11 ice

D FIGURE SKATING
12 figure skater
13 figure skate
14 blade

E CROSS-COUNTRY SKIING
15 skier
16 track

F BOBSLEDDING
17 helmet
18 bobsleigh

G SNOWMOBILING
19 snowmobile

Cross-country skiing is slower than downhill skiing.

Bobsledding is more exciting than figure skating.

A: Figure skating is more difficult than
....

A: .... is ....
.... than ....

Questions for discussion
1 Do people do these sports in your country?
2 Which of these sports needs a hill?

1 lift
2 weights
3 mat
4 run
5 running machine/treadmill
6 exercise bike
7 aerobics
8 rowing machine
9 skip
10 skipping rope
11 throw (a ball)
12 catch (a ball)
13 stretch
14 bend over
15 reach
16 walk
17 hop
18 bounce (a ball)

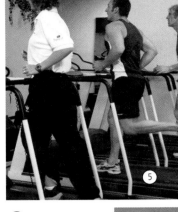

19 kick (a ball)
20 kneel
21 fall
22 do sit-ups
23 do press-ups
24 do a handstand

What's he doing? (13)
He's stretching.

What are they doing? (4)
They're running.

A: What's he/she doing?/What are they doing?
B: He's ..../They're ....

Questions for discussion
Which of these actions do you do in:
1 football?
2 tennis?

A CLASSICAL CONCERT

1 (symphony) orchestra
2 audience
3 (sheet) music
4 music stand
5 conductor

B BALLET

6 ballerina
7 ballet dancer
8 ballet shoe

C THEATRE

9 spotlight
10 aisle
11 actor

D OPERA

12 stage set
13 chorus
14 singer
15 stage
16 orchestra pit
17 podium

E ROCK CONCERT

18 band
19 singer/vocalist

F CINEMA

20 film, movie *AmE*

When did you last go to the theatre?
I went two months ago.

When did you last go to an opera?
I've never been.

A: **When did you last go to a/the** ....?
B: I went .... ago./ I've never been.

Questions for discussion
Do you know any famous singers/actors?

HOBBIES

1 coin collecting
2 (coin) album
3 coin
4 stamp collecting
5 (stamp) album
6 magnifying glass
7 photography
8 camera
9 astronomy
10 telescope
11 home improvement/DIY
12 bird-watching
13 binoculars
14 gardening
15 cookery

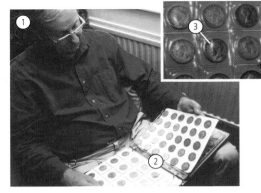

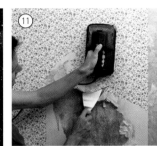

CRAFTS

16 sculpture
17 sculpture
18 embroidery
19 spinning
20 knitting
21 knitting needle
22 sewing machine
23 sewing
24 painting
25 brushes
26 pottery
27 potter's wheel
28 woodworking

GAMES

1 video/computer games
2 Scrabble™
3 chess
4 board
5 pieces
6 dice
7 draughts
8 Monopoly™
9 backgammon
10 cards

Do you like playing chess?
Yes, I do.

Do you like knitting?
I've never tried it.

A: Do you like painting?
B: ....

A: Do you like ....ing?
B: Yes, I do./No, I don't./I've never tried it.

Questions for discussion

1 Which of the crafts do you think is the most difficult?

2 Which of these games can you play?

MUSICAL INSTRUMENTS

STRINGS

1 bow
2 violin
3 viola
4 double bass
5 cello
6 piano

BRASS

7 French horn
8 tuba
9 trumpet
10 trombone

WOODWIND

11 flute
12 piccolo
13 oboe
14 recorder
15 clarinet
16 saxophone
17 bassoon

PERCUSSION

18 xylophone
19 drum kit
20 cymbal
21 drum

OTHER INSTRUMENTS

22 accordion
23 harmonica

POP MUSIC

24 mike (microphone)
25 electric guitar
26 bass guitar
27 keyboards
28 amplifier

A double bass is larger than a cello.

A piano is more expensive than a harmonica.

A: Drums are louder than ....

A: A .... is heavier than a flute.

A: A/An .... is .... er/ more .... than a/an ....

Questions for discussion

1 Can you play any of these instruments?
2 Which instrument has the nicest sound?
3 Which instruments can be very loud?

1 sea, ocean *AmE*
2 pier
3 deckchair
4 promenade
5 beach towel
6 windbreak
7 shade
8 (beach) umbrella
9 sandcastle
10 sunbather
11 life guard
12 sand
13 bucket, pail *AmE*
14 spade

15 shell
16 bikini
17 swimming costume
18 swimming trunks
19 wave
20 surfer
21 surfboard

22 beach ball
23 Li-lo™/air bed
24 sunglasses
25 sunscreen

What's this? (6)
It's a windbreak.

What are these? (24)
They're sunglasses.

A: What's this? (19)
B: It's ....

A: What's this?/What are these?
B: It's a/an ..../They're
....

Questions for discussion
1 Which of these things can you take in the sea with you?
2 What do you usually take when you go to a beach?

IN THE COUNTRY

A **BALLOONING**

1 hot-air balloon

B **BOATING HOLIDAY**

2 barge
3 canal
4 angler
5 fishing rod
6 fishing hook

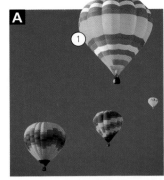

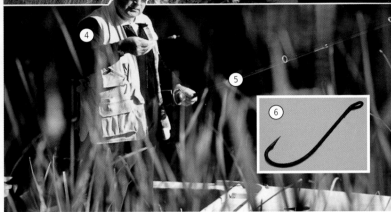

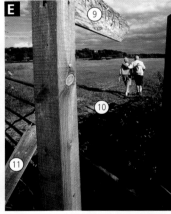

C **PONY-TREKKING**

D **HIKING**

7 hiker
8 rucksack

E **RAMBLING**

9 signpost
10 path
11 stile
12 nature reserve

F **CAMPING**

13 caravan site
14 campsite
15 picnic
16 camper
17 tent
18 camping stove
19 groundsheet
20 walking boot
21 sleeping bag

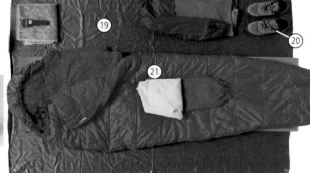

Are you going to go camping next summer?
Yes, I am.

No, I'm not.

A: Are you going to go ....ing next summer?

B: ....

Questions for discussion

1 Do you like any of these activities?
2 Which of these activities would you never do?

1 theme park
2 roller coaster
3 ride
4 carnival

5 exhibition
6 bookshop
7 museum
8 zoo
9 botanical garden
10 safari park/wildlife park
11 craft fair

12 queue, line *AmE*
13 tour guide
14 tourist
15 church
16 church tower
17 castle

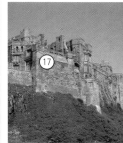

18 village
19 stately home
20 city wall
21 park

Would you rather go to an exhibition or a craft fair?
I'd rather go to a craft fair.

Neither. I'd rather visit a zoo.

A: Would you rather go to/visit a/an .... or a/an ....?
B: I'd rather go to/visit a/an ....

Questions for discussion
1 Which of these places are historical?
2 Are there any of these places near your home?

13.1 PETS

1 cat
2 fur
3 whiskers
4 basket
5 kitten
6 paw
7 hamster
8 rabbit
9 cage
10 budgerigar/budgie
11 gerbil
12 tail
13 hutch

14 fish tank
15 tropical fish
16 guinea pig
17 (goldfish) bowl
18 goldfish
19 pony
20 puppy
21 kennel
22 dog

Have you got any pets?
No, I haven't.
Yes, I have. I've got a dog and some goldfish.

A: Have you got any pets?
B: ....

Questions for discussion
1 Which of these pets live in a cage or hutch?
2 Which of these pets could you keep in a flat?
3 Which of these pets need to be outdoors?

1 donkey
2 (nanny) goat
3 kid
4 (billy) goat
5 turkey
6 bull
7 cow
8 calf
9 rabbit
10 sheep
11 lamb
12 goose
13 gosling
14 duck
15 duckling

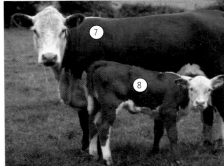

16	chicken	20	foal
17	cockerel	21	chick
18	ram	22	pig
19	horse	23	piglet

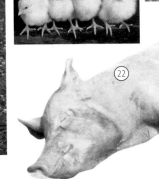

What is a young pig called?
It's called a piglet.

What is a young sheep called?
It's called a lamb.

A: **What is a young** ....
    called?
B: It's called a ....

Questions for discussion
1 Which of these words only refer to male animals?
2 Which of these animals produce milk for their young?

1 elephant
2 trunk
3 tusk
4 lion
5 mane
6 tiger
7 bear
8 rhinoceros
9 horn
10 hippopotamus
11 kangaroo
12 pouch
13 cheetah
14 buffalo
15 zebra
16 stripes
17 koala bear
18 giraffe
19 leopard
20 spots
21 deer
22 antlers

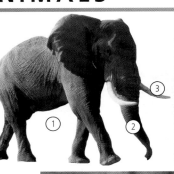

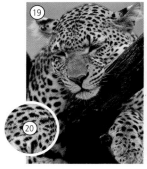

23 llama
24 gorilla
25 tortoise
26 polar bear
27 fox
28 camel
29 hump
30 monkey
31 lizard
32 frog
33 badger
34 alligator
35 crocodile
36 snake

FISH

1 shark
2 tail
3 gills
4 fin
5 snout
6 trout

7 scales
8 angelfish
9 eel
10 sunfish

SEA ANIMALS

11 whale
12 seal
13 walrus
14 tusk
15 dolphin
16 flipper
17 shrimp
18 crab
19 octopus
20 tentacle
21 clam

22 starfish
23 turtle
24 lobster
25 claw
26 mussels

Which is smaller – an octopus or a whale?
An octopus.

Which is more friendly – a dolphin or a shark?
A dolphin.

A: **Which is slower – a shark or a walrus?**

B: ....

Questions for discussion

1 Which of the fish do people often eat?
2 Which of the sea animals can you sometimes find on land?

1 flamingo
2 pelican
3 crane
4 robin
5 penguin
6 flipper
7 cockatoo
8 crest
9 owl
10 swallow
11 ostrich
12 eagle
13 beak
14 falcon
15 pheasant
16 tail
17 stork

18 gull
19 hummingbird
20 pigeon
21 nest
22 egg

23 bluejay
24 peacock
25 feathers
26 parrot
27 swan
28 bill
29 wings
30 crow
31 claws

What do robins look like?
They're small, with brown and red feathers.

What do swans look like?
They're white, with long necks.

A: **What do flamingos look like?**
B: They're .... with ....

A: **What do** .... **look like?**
B: They're .... with ....

Questions for discussion
1 Which of these birds eat meat?
2 Which of these birds can't fly?
3 Which of these birds live in your country?

INSECTS

1 wasp nest
2 wasp
3 mosquito
4 cockroach
5 beehive
6 moth
7 caterpillar
8 ladybird
9 butterfly
10 dragonfly
11 bee
12 honeycomb
13 grasshopper
14 spider
15 web
16 ant
17 fly

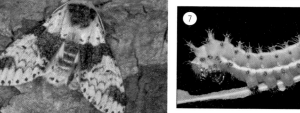

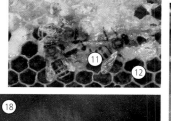

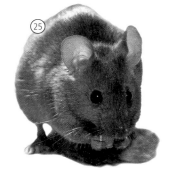

SMALL ANIMALS

18 red squirrel
19 rat
20 mole
21 toad
22 snail
23 hedgehog
24 spines
25 mouse

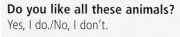

Do you like all these animals?
Yes, I do./No, I don't.

Which ones don't you like?
I don't like flies or mice.

A: **Do you like all these animals?**
B: ....

A: **Which ones don't you like?**
B: ....

Questions for discussion
1 Which of these animals do you like?
2 Which of these animals can you sometimes find in the house?

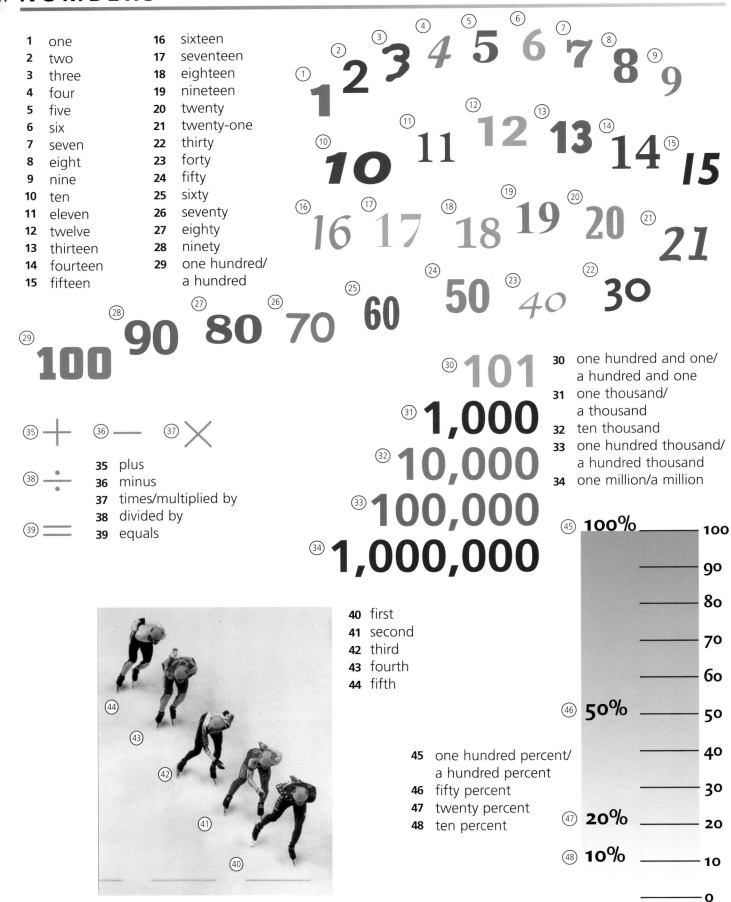

1 one
2 two
3 three
4 four
5 five
6 six
7 seven
8 eight
9 nine
10 ten
11 eleven
12 twelve
13 thirteen
14 fourteen
15 fifteen

16 sixteen
17 seventeen
18 eighteen
19 nineteen
20 twenty
21 twenty-one
22 thirty
23 forty
24 fifty
25 sixty
26 seventy
27 eighty
28 ninety
29 one hundred/
a hundred

35 plus
36 minus
37 times/multiplied by
38 divided by
39 equals

30 one hundred and one/
a hundred and one
31 one thousand/
a thousand
32 ten thousand
33 one hundred thousand/
a hundred thousand
34 one million/a million

40 first
41 second
42 third
43 fourth
44 fifth

45 one hundred percent/
a hundred percent
46 fifty percent
47 twenty percent
48 ten percent

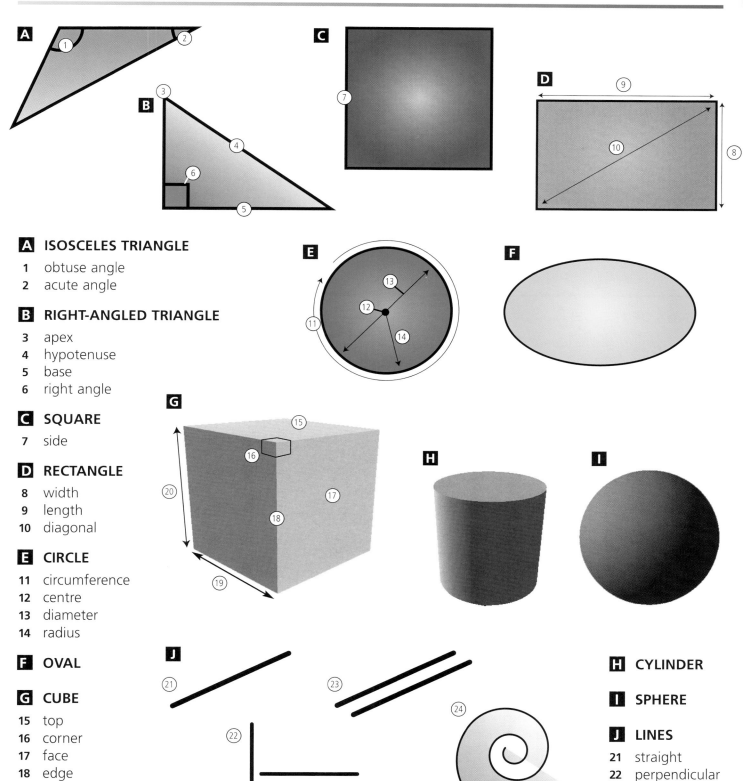

A ISOSCELES TRIANGLE
1 obtuse angle
2 acute angle

B RIGHT-ANGLED TRIANGLE
3 apex
4 hypotenuse
5 base
6 right angle

C SQUARE
7 side

D RECTANGLE
8 width
9 length
10 diagonal

E CIRCLE
11 circumference
12 centre
13 diameter
14 radius

F OVAL

G CUBE
15 top
16 corner
17 face
18 edge
19 depth
20 height

H CYLINDER

I SPHERE

J LINES
21 straight
22 perpendicular
23 parallel
24 spiral

What's the diameter of the circle? (13)
It's about 3 centimetres.

What's the length of the line? (21)
It's about 3 centimetres.

A: What's the .... of the
......................?
B: It's about .... centimetres.

Questions for discussion

Give your partner instructions. He/She must draw the shapes that you describe. Give measurements.

A MONTHS

JANUARY	FEBRUARY	MARCH	APRIL	MAY	JUNE
S M T W T F S	S M T W T F S	S M T W T F S	S M T W T F S	S M T W T F S	S M T W T F S
1 2 3 4 5 6	1 2 3	1 2 3	1 2 3 4 5 6 7	1 2 3 4 5	1 2
7 8 9 10 11 12 13	4 5 6 7 8 9 10	4 5 6 7 8 9 10	8 9 10 11 12 13 14	6 7 8 9 10 11 12	3 4 5 6 7 8 9
14 15 16 17 18 19 20	11 12 13 14 15 16 17	11 12 13 14 15 16 17	15 16 17 18 19 20 21	13 14 15 16 17 18 19	10 11 12 13 14 15 16
21 22 23 24 25 26 27	18 19 20 21 22 23 24	18 19 20 21 22 23 24	22 23 24 25 26 27 28	20 21 22 23 24 25 26	17 18 19 20 21 22 23
28 29 30 31	25 26 27 28	25 26 27 28 29 30 31	29 30	27 28 29 30 31	24 25 26 27 28 29 30

JULY	AUGUST	SEPTEMBER	OCTOBER	NOVEMBER	DECEMBER
S M T W T F S	S M T W T F S	S M T W T F S	S M T W T F S	S M T W T F S	S M T W T F S
1 2 3 4 5 6 7	1 2 3 4	1	1 2 3 4 5 6	1 2 3	1
8 9 10 11 12 13 14	5 6 7 8 9 10 11	2 3 4 5 6 7 8	7 8 9 10 11 12 13	4 5 6 7 8 9 10	2 3 4 5 6 7 8
15 16 17 18 19 20 21	12 13 14 15 16 17 18	9 10 11 12 13 14 15	14 15 16 17 18 19 20	11 12 13 14 15 16 17	9 10 11 12 13 14 15
22 23 24 25 26 27 28	19 20 21 22 23 24 25	16 17 18 19 20 21 22	21 22 23 24 25 26 27	18 19 20 21 22 23 24	16 17 18 19 20 21 22
29 30 31	26 27 28 29 30 31	23 24 25 26 27 28 29	28 29 30 31	25 26 27 28 29 30	23 24 25 26 27 28 29
		30			30 31

B DAYS OF THE WEEK

October

Monday	Tuesday	Wednesday	Thursday	Friday	Saturday	Sunday
1	2	3	4	5	6	
7	8	9	10	11	12	13
14	15	16	17	18	19	20
21	22	23	24	25	26	27

C FESTIVALS

1 Easter Day*
2 Mother's Day*
3 Halloween (October 31st)
4 May Day (May 1st)
5 Bonfire Night/Guy Fawkes' Night (November 5th)
6 Father's Day*
7 St Valentine's Day (February 14th)
8 Christmas Day (December 25th)
9 New Year's Eve (December 31st)

* the date changes from year to year

When's May Day?
It's on May the first.

When's Christmas Day?
It's in December.

A: **When's Halloween?**
B: ....

A: **When's** ....?
B: It's on (date)./It's in (month).

Questions for discussion

1 Which of these are religious festivals?
2 Which festivals do you celebrate in your country? When are they?

1 clock
2 hour hand
3 minute hand
4 face
5 (digital) watch
6 (analogue) watch

12 seven fifteen/(a) quarter past seven
13 seven twenty/twenty past seven
14 seven thirty/half past seven
15 seven thirty-five/twenty-five to eight
16 seven forty/twenty to eight
17 seven forty-five/(a) quarter to eight
18 seven fifty/ten to eight
19 seven fifty-five/five to eight
20 eight am/eight (o'clock) in the morning
21 eight pm/eight (o'clock) in the evening

7 twelve o'clock (midnight)
8 twelve o'clock (noon/midday)
9 seven (o'clock)
10 seven o five/five past seven
11 seven ten/ten past seven

Cambridge ➡ London

MONDAY TO FRIDAY									
Cambridge	10.00	11.00	12.00	13.00	15.00	16.30	18.00	19.30	....	22.30
London	11.30	12.30	13.30	14.45	16.30	18.00	19.30	21.00	....	24.00
SATURDAY									
Cambridge	10.15	11.00	12.15	....	15.00	....	18.15	....	22.15	....
London	11.45	12.30	13.45	....	16.30	....	19.45	....	23.45	....
SUNDAY									
Cambridge	....	11.00	....	13.30	....	17.00	....	20.00	....	22.15
London	....	12.30	....	15.00	....	18.30	....	21.30	....	23.45

22 eleven hundred hours
23 twelve hundred hours
24 thirteen hundred hours
25 fifteen hundred hours
26 eighteen hundred hours
27 nineteen thirty
28 nineteen forty-five
29 twenty-four hundred hours

What time does the first train leave?
It leaves at ten o'clock.

What time does the first train arrive?
It arrives at half past eleven.

A: **What time does the ....**
   train leave/arrive?
B: It leaves/arrives at ....

Questions for discussion
1 What time is it?
2 What time do you usually get up/go to bed?

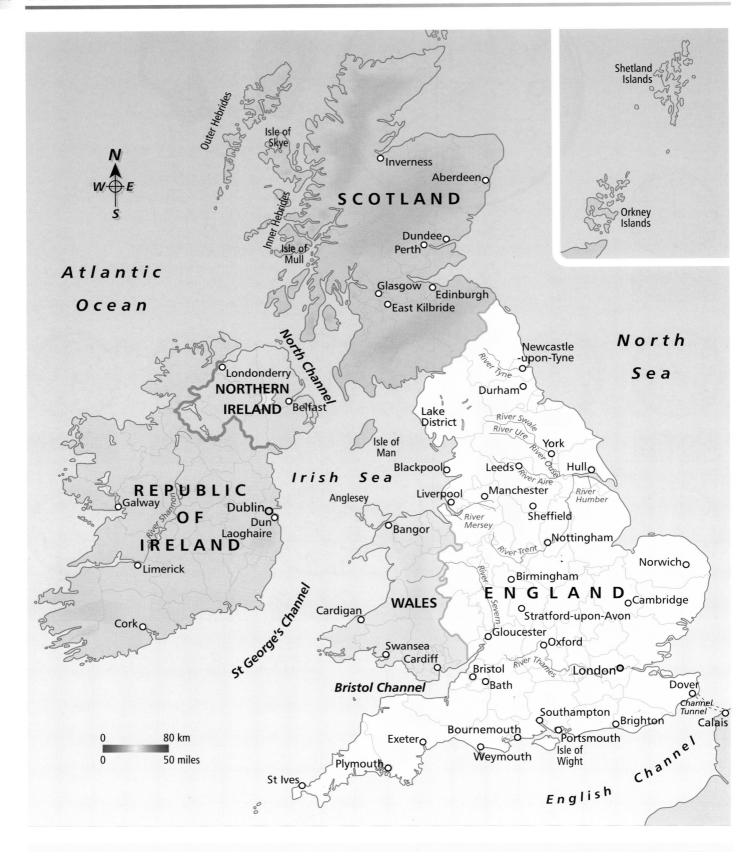

Where's Bristol?
It's in the west of England.

Where's Inverness?
It's in the north of Scotland.

A: **Where's Belfast?**
B: ....

A: **Where's** ....?
B: It's in the .... of ....

Questions for discussion
1 Which of these cities are capital cities?
2 Which of these places would you like to visit?

ALASKA
CANADA

New England
Middle Atlantic States/The East Coast
Southern States/The South
Southwestern States/The Southwest
Midwestern States/The Midwest
Rocky Mountain States
Pacific Coast States/The West Coast

CANADA

Seattle
WASHINGTON
Portland
OREGON
Boise
IDAHO
MONTANA
Helena
NORTH DAKOTA
Bismarck
SOUTH DAKOTA
Pierre
MINNESOTA
Minneapolis
WISCONSIN
Milwaukee
MICHIGAN
Lake Superior
Lake Huron
Lake Michigan
Lake Ontario
Lake Erie
Detroit
Cleveland
OHIO
Chicago
NEW HAMPSHIRE
VERMONT
MAINE
Augusta
Concord
MASSACHUSETTS
NEW YORK
Boston
Buffalo
New York
RHODE ISLAND
CONNECTICUT
NEW JERSEY
Philadelphia
PENNSYLVANIA
DELAWARE
MARYLAND
WASHINGTON, DC
Carson City
NEVADA
Sacramento
San Francisco
CALIFORNIA
Sierra Nevada Mountains
Las Vegas
Los Angeles
San Diego
Great Salt Lake
Salt Lake City
UTAH
WYOMING
Cheyenne
NEBRASKA
Omaha
IOWA
Denver
COLORADO
Kansas City
KANSAS
St Louis
MISSOURI
Louisville
KENTUCKY
Nashville
INDIANA
Indianapolis
Cincinnati
ILLINOIS
WEST VIRGINIA
VIRGINIA
Norfolk
Appalachian Mountains
Grand Canyon
Albuquerque
Santa Fe
NEW MEXICO
ARIZONA
Phoenix
Tucson
El Paso
Oklahoma City
OKLAHOMA
Memphis
ARKANSAS
Little Rock
TENNESSEE
NORTH CAROLINA
Charlotte
SOUTH CAROLINA
Charleston
Atlanta
GEORGIA
Birmingham
ALABAMA
Jackson
MISSISSIPPI
Dallas
Odessa
TEXAS
Austin
San Antonio
Houston
LOUISIANA
New Orleans
Tallahassee
Jacksonville
FLORIDA
Tampa
Miami
Rocky Mountains
Pacific Ocean
Atlantic Ocean
Mississippi River
Missouri River
Gulf of Mexico
MEXICO
HAWAII

400 km
250 miles

N north
S south
E east
W west

Where's Alabama?
It's east of Mississippi and west of Georgia.

Where's Kansas?
It's south of Nebraska and north of Oklahoma.

A: Where's Indiana?
B: ....

A: **Where's ....?**
B: It's .... of ....
and .... of ....

Questions for discussion
1 Which of the states have a sea coast?
2 Which of the states are on a lake?
3 Which of the states have a border with another country?

1 peak
2 mountain
3 lake
4 cactus
5 meadow
6 hill
7 valley
8 acorn
9 oak tree
10 palm tree
11 desert
12 (sand) dune
13 reservoir
14 dam
15 fir tree
16 fir cone
17 forest
18 island
19 coastline
20 pond
21 wood
22 waterfall
23 stream/brook

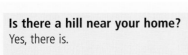

24 rock
25 cliff
26 grass
27 canal
28 cave
29 beach
30 river
31 field
32 chestnut tree
33 conkers

Is there a hill near your home?
Yes, there is.

Are there any fields near your home?
No, there aren't.

A: **Is there a/Are there any** ....
 near ....?
B: Yes, there is./No, there isn't./
 Yes, there are./No, there aren't.

Questions for discussion
What's the difference between:
1 a hill and a mountain?
2 a river and a lake?

SEASONS

1 summer
2 autumn, fall *AmE*
3 winter
4 spring

WEATHER

5 rainy
6 sunny
7 snowy
8 icy
9 clear
10 cloudy/overcast
11 foggy
12 hazy

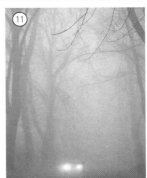

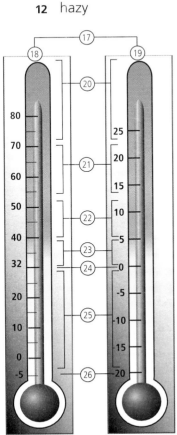

13 windy
14 stormy
15 lightning and thunder
16 rainbow

TEMPERATURE

17 thermometer
18 degrees Fahrenheit
19 degrees Celsius/degrees Centigrade
20 hot
21 warm
22 cool/chilly
23 cold
24 freezing
25 below freezing
26 five (degrees) below (zero)/minus twenty degrees

What's the weather like?
It's foggy.

What's the weather like?
It's cloudy and cool.

A: **What's the weather like? (5) (23)**
B: It's .... and ....

A: **What's the weather like?**
B: It's ....

Questions for discussion
What's the weather like in your country:
1 in spring/winter/summer?
2 today?

HE PLANETS

1 Mercury
2 Venus
3 Earth
4 Mars
5 Jupiter
6 Saturn
7 Uranus
8 Neptune
9 Pluto

10 sun
11 solar system

12 orbit
13 star
14 constellation
15 comet
16 satellite
17 galaxy
18 new moon
19 half moon
20 full moon
21 moon

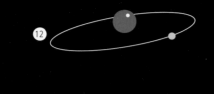

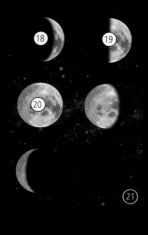

22 fuel tank
23 booster rocke
24 space shuttle
25 launch pad
26 astronaut
27 space suit
28 flag
29 lunar module
30 lunar vehicle

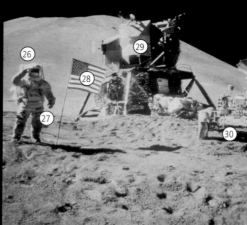

Which planet is the largest?
Jupiter

Which planet is the most distant from Earth?
Pluto

A: Which planet is the nearest to Earth?
B: ....

A: Which planet is the ....
est/the most ....?
B: ....

Questions for discussion

1 Do you know any constellations?
2 Have you ever seen a comet?
3 Which planets has man explored?

A HARDWARE

1 scanner
2 personal computer/PC
3 CD-ROM drive
4 A drive/floppy disk drive
5 C drive/hard disk drive
6 monitor
7 display screen
8 keyboard
9 printer
10 mouse mat
11 mouse
12 laptop
13 CD-Rom
14 console
15 gamepad
16 joystick
17 floppy disk/diskette
18 electronic/computer game

B SOFTWARE

19 word processor
20 menu bar
21 toolbar
22 document
23 spreadsheet
24 table
25 folder

26 file
27 cursor
28 font
29 window
30 icon

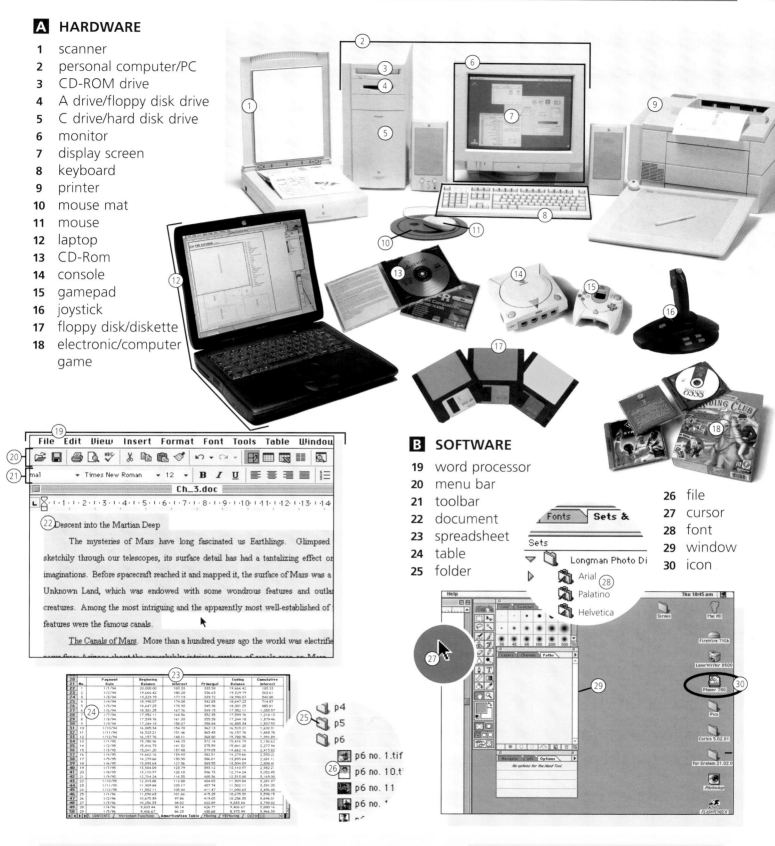

What's a printer used for?
It's used for printing documents.

What's a diskette used for?
It's used for storing information.

A: **What's a joystick used for?**
B: It's used for ....

A: **What's a .... used for?**
B: It's used for ....

Questions for discussion
1 Do you use a computer at home or at work?
2 What does it look like?

THE WORLD WIDE WEB

1 web browser [e.g. Microsoft Internet Explorer™]
2 Internet service provider [e.g. AOL™]
3 password
4 Internet café
5 keyword
6 search engine [e.g. Yahoo™]
7 search page
8 hyperlink
9 website
10 web address (URL)
11 home page

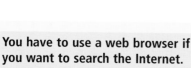

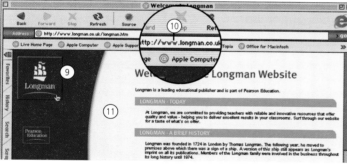

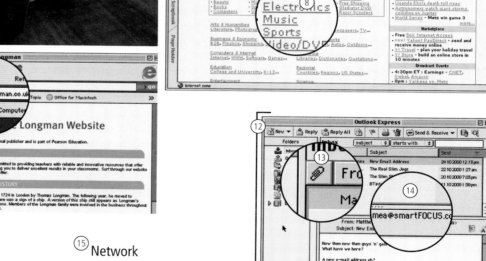

E-MAIL

12 e-mail software [e.g. Outlook Express™]
13 file attachment
14 e-mail address
15 network
16 server

15 Network

Server

Computers

You have to use a web browser if you want to search the Internet.

You have to know the web address if you want to find a website.

A: You have to .... if you want to ....

Questions for discussion

1 How often do you use the Internet?
2 What do you use it for?
3 Do you ever have any problems?

1 clock-radio
2 (video) cassette
3 DVD player
4 DVD/digital versatile disc
5 satellite TV/cable TV
6 television/TV
7 screen
8 video cassette recorder/VCR

9 games console
10 stereo system/hi-fi
11 compact disc player
12 tuner
13 tape deck/cassette deck
14 speaker
15 compact disc/CD
16 remote control
17 computer
18 electric typewriter
19 personal cassette player/Walkman™
20 headphones
21 (audio) cassette/tape
22 tape recorder/cassette player
23 radio

1 (tele)phone
2 answering machine
3 keypad
4 charger
5 mobile, cell phone *AmE*
6 text message
7 cordless phone
8 base

9 pager
10 electronic personal organiser/PDA
11 pocket calculator

12 flash
13 film
14 lens
15 (still) camera
16 digital camera
17 Polaroid™ camera
18 video camera
19 slide projector
20 slides

21 torch
22 battery
23 light bulb

Will we all have a mobile phone in 2050?
Yes, we will.

Will cameras still need a film in 2050?
No, they won't.

A: **Will** .... (still) .... **in 2050?**
B: Yes, we/it/they will./No, we/it/they won't.

Questions for discussion
1 Which of these things do you have?
2 Which of these things would you like to have?

FEELINGS

1 miserable
2 sad
3 pleased
4 happy
5 ecstatic
6 annoyed
7 angry
8 furious
9 nervous
10 suspicious
11 scared/afraid
12 shy
13 surprised
14 confused
15 bored

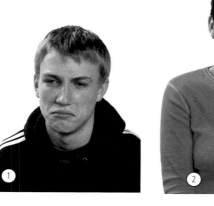

Is she happy? (4)
Yes, she is.

Does she look nervous? (15)
No, she doesn't.

A: Is he/she ....?
B: Yes, he/she is./No, he/she isn't.

A: Does he/she look ....?
B: Yes, he/she does./No, he/she doesn't.

Questions for discussion

How do you feel in these situations?

1 you have an interview
2 someone gives you a present to say 'thank you'

OPPOSITES

1 neat/tidy
2 messy/untidy

3 dry
4 wet

5 tight
6 loose

7 heavy
8 light

9 open
10 closed

11 short
12 long

13 empty
14 full

15 rough
16 smooth

17 near/close
18 far

19 dark
20 light

21 thin
22 thick

23 narrow
24 wide

25 hard
26 soft

27 cheap
28 expensive

29 deep
30 shallow

31 fast
32 slow

£1.05
£150.00

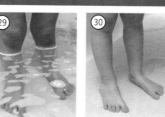
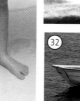

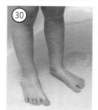

Is it soft? (26)
Yes, it is.

Is it light? (7)
No, it isn't. It's heavy.

A: **Is it full? (13)**
B: ....

A: **Is it** ....?
B: Yes, it is./No, it isn't. It's ....

Questions for discussion
Describe the clothes you are wearing using as many of these adjectives as possible.

1 from
2 to

3 in front of
4 behind

5 over
6 under

7 in
8 out

9 up
10 down

11 onto
12 off

13 on
14 off

15 above
16 below

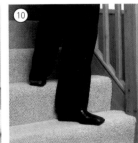

Where is he standing? (4)
He's standing behind the girl.

Where is she climbing? (11)
She's climbing onto the table.

A: **Where is he/she/it standing/sitting/going?**
B: He's/She's/It's standing/sitting/going
....

Questions for discussion

Describe your position in the room using as many of these prepositions as possible.

PREPOSITIONS 2

1 round
2 between
3 against
4 across
5 away from
6 towards
7 outside
8 inside
9 into
10 through
11 out of

12 along
13 beside/next to
14 at the top
15 in the middle
16 at the bottom
17 on top of
18 under/underneath

Where is he? (17)
He's on top of the table.

Where are they? (13)
They're next to each other.

A: **Where is she/he/it?/Where are they?**
B: He/She/It's ..../They're
....

Questions for discussion
1 What is outside the room that you're in at the moment?
2 Is anyone sitting beside you?

A drive/floppy disk drive
/'eɪ draɪv, ˌflɒpi 'dɪsk ˌdraɪv/ **109**
A-Level/Higher Grade
/'eɪ ˌlevəl, 'haɪə ˌgreɪd/ **50**
Aberdeen /ˌæbə'diːn/ **104**
above /ə'bʌv/ **115**
accelerator /ək'seləreɪtər/ **67**
accessories /ək'sesəriz/ **49**
accordion /ə'kɔːdiən/ **90**
accountant /ə'kaʊntənt/ **23**
acorn /'eɪkɔːn/ **106**
across /ə'krɒs/ **116**
actor /'æktər/ **87**
acute angle /ə'kjuːt ˌæŋgəl/ **101**
add /æd/ **63**
address /ə'dres‖'ædres/ **4, 76**
adjustable spanner
/əˌdʒʌstəbəl 'spænər/ **26**
adult /'ædʌlt, ə'dʌlt/ **4**
aerobics /eə'rəʊbɪks/ **86**
afraid /ə'freɪd/ **113**
aftershave /'ɑːftəʃeɪv/ **37**
against /ə'genst/ **116**
age /eɪdʒ/ **4**
air bed /'eə bed/ **91**
airer /'eərər/ **15**
air filter /'eə ˌfɪltər/ **66**
airing cupboard /'eərɪŋ ˌkʌbəd/ **18**
airmail letter /'eəmeɪl ˌletər/ **76**
air steward /'eə ˌstjuːəd/ **71**
air tank /'eə tæŋk/ **84**
air traffic controller
/eə 'træfɪk kənˌtrəʊlər/ **71**
aisle /aɪl/ **57, 82**
aisle seat /'aɪl siːt/ **71**
Alabama /ˌælə'bæmə/ **105**
alarm clock /ə'lɑːm klɒk/ **11**
Alaska /ə'læskə/ **105**
Alka Seltzer™ /ˌælkə 'seltsər/ **39**
allergy /'ælədʒi/ **39**
alligator /'ælɪgeɪtər/ **96**
along /ə'lɒŋ/ **116**
alphabet board /'ælfəbet ˌbɔːd/ **42**
aluminium foil
/ˌæljumɪniəm 'fɔɪl/ **8**
amber /'æmbər/ **68**
ambulance /'æmbjʊləns/ **79**
ambulance service
/'æmbjʊləns ˌsɜːvɪs/ **79**
amethyst /'æmɪθɪst/ **49**
amplifier /'æmplɪfaɪər/ **90**
anaesthetist /ə'niːsθətɪst/ **41**
analogue watch
/'ænəlɒg wɒtʃ/ **103**
anchor /'æŋkər/ **72**
angelfish /'eɪndʒəlˌfɪʃ/ **97**
angler /'æŋglər/ **92**
Anglesey /'æŋgəlsiː/ **104**
angry /'æŋgri/ **113**
ankle /'æŋkəl/ **31**
ankle socks /'.. ./ **44**
annoyed /ə'nɔɪd/ **113**
answer the phone
/ˌɑːnsə ðə 'fəʊn/ **25**
answering machine
/'ɑːnsərɪŋ məˌʃiːn/ **112**
ant /ænt/ **99**

antacid /ænt'æsɪd/ **39**
antihistamine tablets
/ˌæntɪ'hɪstəmiːn ˌtæbləts/ **39**
antlers /'æntləz/ **96**
apex /'eɪpeks/ **101**
Appalachian Mountains
/ˌæpəleɪtʃiən 'maʊntənz/ **105**
apple /'æpəl/ **56**
apple pie /æpəl 'paɪ/ **60**
application /ˌæplɪ'keɪʃən/ **109**
application form
/ˌæplɪ'keɪʃən fɔːm/ **20**
apricot /'eɪprɪkɒt/ **56**
April /'eɪprəl/ **102**
archer /'ɑːtʃər/ **83**
archery /'ɑːtʃəri/ **83**
architect /'ɑːkɪtekt/ **23**
Arizona /ˌærɪ'zəʊnə/ **105**
Arkansas /'ɑːkənsɔː/ **105**
arm /ɑːm/ **31**
armchair /'ɑːmtʃeər/ **12**
armrest /'ɑːmrest/ **71**
arrow /'ærəʊ/ **83**
art /ɑːt/ **53**
artery /'ɑːtəri/ **32**
artichoke /'ɑːtɪtʃəʊk/ **55**
articulated lorry
/ɑːˌtɪkjʊleɪtɪd 'lɒri/ **66**
artist /'ɑːtɪst/ **23**
asparagus /ə'spærəgəs/ **55**
assembly line /ə'sembli laɪn/ **27**
assistant /ə'sɪstənt/ **36**
astronaut /'æstrənɔːt/ **108**
astronomy /ə'strɒnəmi/ **88**
Atlanta /ət'læntə/ **105**
Atlantic Ocean
/ətˌlæntɪk 'əʊʃən/ **105**
atlas /'ætləs/ **54**
attachment /ə'tætʃmənt/ **110**
attacker /ə'tækər/ **80**
at the bottom
/ət ðə 'bɒtəm/ **116**
at the top /ət ðə 'tɒp/ **116**
attic /'ætɪk/ **21**
aubergine /'əʊbəʒiːn/ **55**
audience /'ɔːdiəns/ **87**
audio cassette/tape
/'ɔːdiəʊ kəˌset, 'ɔːdiəʊ ˌteɪp/ **111**
August /'ɔːgəst/ **102**
aunt /ɑːnt/ **5**
autumn /'ɔːtəm/ **107**
avocado /ˌævə'kɑːdəʊ/ **56**
away from /ə'weɪ frəm/ **116**
axe /æks/ **26**

baby /'beɪbi/ **4**
baby bottle /'.. ˌ../ **14**
baby carrier /'beɪbi ˌkæriər/ **14**
baby clothes /'beɪbi kləʊðz/ **14**
baby cup /'.. ./ **14**
baby wipes /'beɪbi waɪps/ **14**
Bachelor of Arts (BA) /ˌbætʃələr əv 'ɑːts, ˌbiː 'eɪ/ **50**
Bachelor of Science (BS)
/ˌbætʃələr əv 'saɪəns, ˌbiː 'es/ **50**
back /bæk/ **31**

backache /'bækeɪk/ **38**
backboard /'bækbɔːd/ **81**
backbone /'bækbəʊn/ **32**
backgammon /'bækgæmən/ **89**
back teeth /bæk 'tiːθ/ **42**
bacon /'beɪkən/ **59**
badger /'bædʒər/ **96**
badminton /'bædmɪntən/ **82**
badminton player /'... ˌ../ **82**
badminton racket
/'bædmɪntən ˌrækɪt/ **82**
bag /bæg/ **62**
bagel /'beɪgəl/ **59**
baggage /'bægɪdʒ/ **70**
baggage carousel
/'bægɪdʒ kærəˌsel/ **70**
baggage reclaim area
/'bægɪdʒ rɪkleɪm ˌeəriə/ **70**
baggy /'bægi/ **46**
bag of sweets /ˌ.. '../ **77**
baguette /bæ'get/ **59**
bails /beɪlz/ **80**
bake /beɪk/ **63**
baked beans /ˌbeɪkt 'biːnz/ **57**
baker /'beɪkər/ **21**
bakery /'beɪkəri/ **59**
baking tray /'beɪkɪŋ treɪ/ **9**
balance beam /'bæləns biːm/ **83**
balcony /'bælkəni/ **7**
bald /bɔːld/ **33**
ball /bɔːl/ **80**
ballerina /ˌbælə'riːnə/ **87**
ballet /'bæleɪ‖bæ'leɪ/ **87**
ballet dancer /'bæleɪ ˌdɑːnsər/ **87**
ballet shoe /'bæleɪ ʃuː/ **87**
ball gown /'bɔːl gaʊn/ **44**
ballooning /bə'luːnɪŋ/ **92**
ballpoint pen /ˌbɔːlpɔɪnt 'pen/ **24, 52**
banana /bə'nɑːnəl‖-'næ-/ **56**
band /bænd/ **87**
bank account number
/'bæŋk əkaʊnt ˌnʌmbər/ **73**
bank balance /'bæŋk ˌbæləns/ **73**
bank clerk /'bæŋk klɑːk/ **23, 73**
bank statement
/'bæŋk ˌsteɪtmənt/ **73**
bar /bɑːr/ **29**
barbecue /'bɑːbɪkjuː/ **16, 63**
barge /bɑːdʒ/ **92**
bar of chocolate
/ˌbɑːr əv 'tʃɒklɪt/ **77**
barrier /'bæriər/ **65, 69**
barrister /'bærɪstər/ **22, 30**
base /beɪs/ **37, 101, 112**
baseball cap /'beɪsbɔːl kæp/ **45**
baseline /'beɪslaɪn/ **82**
basin /'beɪsən/ **42**
basket /'bɑːskɪt/ **81, 94**
basketball /'bɑːskɪtbɔːl/ **81**
basketball player /'... ˌ../ **81**
bass guitar /ˌbeɪs gɪ'tɑːr/ **90**
bassoon /bə'suːn/ **90**
bat /bæt/ **80, 82**
bath /bɑːθ/ **10**
bath mat /'bɑːθ mæt/ **10**

bathrobe /'bɑːθrəʊb/ **43**
bathroom /'bɑːθrʊm/ **18, 29**
bathroom cabinet
/ˌbɑːθrʊm 'kæbɪnət/ **10**
bath towel /'. ../ **10**
batsman /'bætsmən/ **80**
battery /'bætəri/ **66, 112**
beach /biːtʃ/ **106**
beach ball /'. ./ **91**
beach towel /'. ../ **91**
beach umbrella /'. .ˌ../ **91**
beak /biːk/ **98**
bear /beər/ **96**
beard /bɪəd/ **33**
beat /biːt/ **63**
beautician /bjuː'tɪʃən/ **36**
bedroom /'bedrʊm/ **18**
bedside table /ˌbedsaɪd 'teɪbəl/ **11**
bedspread /'bedspred/ **11**
bee /biː/ **99**
beefburger /'biːfbɜːgər/ **61**
beehive /'biːhaɪv/ **99**
beef joint /'biːf dʒɔɪnt/ **59**
beer /bɪər/ **58**
beetroot /'biːtruːt/ **55**
behind /bɪ'haɪnd/ **115**
beige /beɪʒ/ **47**
Belfast /'belfɑːst/ **104**
Belisha beacon
/bəˌliːʃə 'biːkən/ **74**
bell tower /'bel ˌtaʊər/ **93**
below /bɪ'ləʊ/ **115**
below freezing /ˌ.ˌ. '../ **107**
belt /belt/ **49**
bench /bentʃ/ **51**
bend over /bend 'əʊvər/ **86**
beside /bɪ'saɪd/ **116**
between /bɪ'twiːn/ **116**
bib /bɪb/ **14**
bicycle /'baɪsɪkəl/ **66, 83**
bike /baɪk/ **83**
bikini /bɪ'kiːni/ **45, 91**
bill /bɪl/ **98**
billboard /'bɪlbɔːd/ **75**
billy goat /'bɪli gəʊt/ **95**
bin /bɪn/ **8, 24**
bin bags /'bɪn bægz/ **58**
binoculars /bɪ'nɒkjʊləz/ **88**
biology /baɪ'ɒlədʒi/ **53**
bird-watching /'bɜːd ˌwɒtʃɪŋ/ **88**
Birmingham /'bɜːmɪŋəm/ **104**
biro™ /'baɪərəʊ/ **24, 77**
birthday card /'bɜːθdeɪ kɑːd/ **76**
biscuits /'bɪskɪts/ **58**
black /blæk/ **47**
black belt /'. ./ **82**
blackboard /'blækbɔːd/ **52**
black cab /blæk 'kæb/ **65**
blackcurrant /ˌblæk'kʌrənt/ **56**
black eye /ˌ. '../ **38**
black hair /ˌ. '../ **33**
blade /bleɪd/ **85**
blender /'blendər/ **9**
blood /blʌd/ **38**
blood pressure gauge
/'blʌd preʃə ˌgeɪdʒ/ **40**
blouse /blaʊz‖blaʊs/ **44**
blow-dry /bləʊ 'draɪ/ **36**

blue /bluː/ **47**
blueberry /'bluːbəri/ **56**
blue cheese /'. ./ **59**
blue-collar worker /. '.. ,../ **23**
bluejay /'bluːˌdʒeɪ/ **98**
blusher /'blʌʃər/ **37**
board /bɔːd/ **89**
boarding pass /'bɔːdɪŋ pɑːs/ **70**
boarding school /'bɔːdɪŋ skuːl/ **50**
boating holiday /'bəʊtɪŋ ˌhɒlɪdi/ **92**
bobsledding /'bɒbsledɪŋ/ **85**
bobsleigh /'bɒbsleɪ/ **85**
boil /bɔɪl/ **63**
boiled egg /ˌbɔɪld 'eg/ **64**
bollard /'bɒləd, -lɑːd/ **74**
bolt /bəʊlt/ **26**
Bonfire Night /'bɒnfaɪə naɪt/ **102**
bonnet /'bɒnɪt/ **67**
book /bʊk/ **51**
bookcase /'bʊk-keɪs/ **12**
books /bʊks/ **12**
bookshop /'bʊkʃɒp/ **78, 93**
booster rocket /'buːstə ˌrɒkɪt/ **108**
boot /buːt/ **67**
boots /buːts/ **43**
border /'bɔːdər/ **16**
bored /bɔːd/ **113**
botanical garden /bəˌtænɪkəl 'gɑːdn/ **93**
bottle /'bɒtl/ **62**
bottle opener /'bɒtl ˌəʊpənər/ **9**
bottled food /ˌbɒtld 'fuːd/ **57**
bounce /baʊns/ **86**
bouncer /'baʊnsər/ **14**
boundary /'baʊndəri/ **80**
bow /baʊ/ **72**
bow /bəʊ/ **83, 90**
bowl /bəʊl/ **13**
bowler /'bəʊlər/ **80**
bow tie /bəʊ 'taɪ/ **45**
box /bɒks/ **62**
boxer /'bɒksər/ **81**
boxer shorts /'.. ,../ **45**
box of chocolates /ˌbɒks əv 'tʃɒklɪts/ **77**
box of tissues /ˌ.. '../ **14**
boxing /'bɒksɪŋ/ **81**
boy /bɔɪ/ **4**
bra /brɑː/ **44**
brace /breɪs/ **42**
bracelet /'breɪslɪt/ **49**
braces /'breɪsɪz/ **49**
bradawl /'brædɔːl/ **26**
brain /breɪn/ **32**
brake /breɪk/ **67**
brake light /'. ./ **67**
brass /brɑːs/ **90**
Brazil nut /brə'zɪl nʌt/ **56**
bread /bred/ **64**
bread roll /. './ **64**
break /breɪk/ **35, 63**
breakfast /'brekfəst/ **64**
breastbone /'brestbəʊn/ **32**
brick /brɪk/ **28**
bricklayer /'brɪkˌleɪər/ **21**

bricks /brɪks/ **51**
bridge /brɪdʒ/ **68, 75**
brie /briː/ **59**
briefcase /'briːfkeɪs/ **29, 49**
Brighton /'braɪtn/ **104**
Bristol /'brɪstl/ **104**
broccoli /'brɒkəli/ **55**
broken leg /ˌbrəʊkən 'leg/ **38**
broken zip /ˌbrəʊkən 'zɪp/ **48**
brooch /brəʊtʃ/ **49**
brook /brʊk/ **106**
broom /bruːm/ **15**
brother /'brʌðər/ **5**
brother-in-law /'brʌðər ɪn lɔː/ **5**
brown /braʊn/ **47**
brown hair /. './ **33**
bruise /bruːz/ **38**
brush /brʌʃ/ **15, 37**
brushes /'brʌʃɪz/ **88**
brush your hair /ˌ. . './
brush your teeth /ˌbrʌʃ jɔː 'tiːθ/ **6**
brussels sprout /ˌbrʌsəlz 'spraʊt/ **55**
bucket /'bʌkɪt/ **15, 91**
buckle /'bʌkəl/ **46, 49**
budgerigar /'bʌdʒərɪgɑːr/ **94**
budgie /'bʌdʒi/ **94**
buffalo /'bʌfələʊ/ **96**
buggy /'bʌgi/ **14**
building blocks /'bɪldɪŋ blɒks/ **51**
bull /bʊl/ **95**
bulldozer /'bʊldəʊzər/ **28**
bumper /'bʌmpər/ **67**
bungalow /'bʌŋgələʊ/ **7**
bunsen burner /ˌbʌnsən 'bɜːnər/ **52**
burgers /'bɜːgəz/ **57**
bus /bʌs/ **65, 68, 74**
bus driver /'bʌs ˌdraɪvər/ **65**
bush /bʊʃ/ **16**
business studies /'bɪznəs ˌstʌdiz/ **53**
bus lane /'bʌs leɪn/ **74**
bus shelter /'bʌs ˌʃeltər/ **74**
bus stop /'bʌs stɒp/ **65, 74**
butcher /'bʊtʃər/ **21**
butter /'bʌtər/ **57, 64**
butterfly /'bʌtəflaɪ/ **99**
butter sauce /'bʌtə sɔːs/ **60**
buttocks /'bʌtəks/ **31**
button /'bʌtn/ **46**
buttonhole /'bʌtnhəʊl/ **46**

C drive /'siː draɪv/ **109**
cabbage /'kæbɪdʒ/ **55**
cabin /'kæbɪn/ **71, 72**
cabin cruiser /'kæbɪn ˌkruːzər/ **72**
cable /'keɪbəl/ **72, 109**
cable TV /ˌkeɪbəl tiː 'viː/ **111**
cactus /'kæktəs/ **106**
cafeteria /ˌkæfə'tɪəriə/ **54**
cafetiere /ˌkæfə'tjeər/ **8**
cage /keɪdʒ/ **94**
cake /keɪk/ **59**
cake stand /'keɪk stænd/ **13**
cake tin /'keɪk tɪn/ **9**
calculator /'kælkjʊleɪtər/ **52**

calendar /'kælɪndər/ **24**
calf /kɑːf‖kæf/ **31**
calf /kɑːf‖kæf/ **95**
California /ˌkælɪ'fɔːnjə/ **105**
calling from a public phone box /ˌkɔːlɪŋ frəm ə ˌpʌblɪk 'fəʊn bɒks/ **79**
Cambridge /'keɪmbrɪdʒ/ **104**
camel /'kæməl/ **96**
camel /'kæməl/ **47**
camera /'kæmərə/ **88**
camper /'kæmpər/ **92**
camping /'kæmpɪŋ/ **92**
camping stove /'kæmpɪŋ stəʊv/ **92**
campsite /'kæmpsaɪt/ **92**
campus /'kæmpəs/ **54**
can /kæn/ **62**
canal /kə'næl/ **92, 106**
candle /'kændl/ **13**
candy AmE /'kændi/ **61**
canoe /kə'nuː/ **84**
canoeing /kə'nuːɪŋ/ **84**
canoeist /kə'nuːɪst/ **84**
captain /'kæptɪn/ **71**
car /kɑːr/ **68**
caravan /'kærəvæn/ **66**
caravan site /'kærəvæn saɪt/ **92**
card /kɑːd/ **76**
Cardiff /'kɑːdɪf/ **104**
cardigan /'kɑːdɪgən/ **43**
Cardigan /'kɑːdɪgən/ **104**
cardiologist /ˌkɑːdi'ɒlədʒɪst/ **40**
cards /kɑːdz/ **89**
cargo /'kɑːgəʊ/ **72**
carnival /'kɑːnɪvəl/ **93**
carpenter /'kɑːpɪntər/ **21**
carpet /'kɑːpɪt/ **11**
carriage /'kærɪdʒ/ **65**
carrier bag /'kæriə bæg/ **57**
carrot /'kærət/ **55**
carrots /'kærəts/ **60**
carry /'kæri/ **34**
cars /kɑːz/ **66**
car seat /'kɑː siːt/ **14**
carton /'kɑːtn/ **62**
cash /kæʃ/ **73**
cashew nut /'kæʃuː nʌt‖kə'ʃuː nʌt/ **56**
cashier /kæ'ʃɪər/ **57, 73**
cashpoint /'kæʃpɔɪnt/ **73**
cashpoint card /'.. . '. / **73**
casserole dish /'kæsərəʊl dɪʃ/ **9**
cassette deck /kə'set dek/ **111**
cassette player /kə'set ˌpleɪər/ **67, 111**
castle /'kɑːsəl/ **93**
casual wear /'kæʒuəl weər/ **44, 45**
cat /kæt/ **94**
catch /kætʃ/ **86**
caterpillar /'kætəˌpɪlər/ **99**
cat food /'kæt fuːd/ **58**
cat's eyes /'. ./ **68**
cauliflower /'kɒliˌflaʊər/ **55**
cave /keɪv/ **106**

CCTV camera /ˌsiː siː tiː viː 'kæmərə/ **74**
CD player /ˌsiː 'diː ˌpleɪər/ **52, 67**
CD-ROM drive /ˌsiː diː 'rɒm draɪv/ **109**
ceiling /'siːlɪŋ/ **18**
celery /'seləri/ **55**
cellar /'selər/ **18**
cello /'tʃeləʊ/ **90**
cell phone AmE /'sel fəʊn/ **112**
cement /sɪ'ment/ **28**
cement mixer /sɪ'ment ˌmɪksər/ **28**
centimetre /'sentɪˌmiːtər/ **62**
central reservation /ˌsentrəl rezə'veɪʃən/ **68**
centre /'sentər/ **101**
centre circle /ˌ.. '../ **80**
cereal /'sɪəriəl/ **58, 64**
chain /tʃeɪn/ **49**
chair /tʃeər/ **13**
chairlift /'tʃeəlɪft/ **85**
chalk /tʃɔːk/ **52**
chambermaid /'tʃeɪmbə'meɪd/ **29**
champagne /ʃæm'peɪn/ **60**
changing mat /'tʃeɪndʒɪŋ mæt/ **14**
charger /'tʃɑːdʒər/ **112**
cheap /tʃiːp/ **114**
checked /tʃekt/ **47**
check-in desk /'tʃek ɪn desk/ **70**
checking in /ˌtʃekɪŋ 'ɪn/ **29**
checking out /ˌtʃekɪŋ 'aʊt/ **29**
check-out area /'tʃek aʊt ˌeəriə/ **57**
checkout desk /'tʃek-aʊt ˌdesk/ **54, 57**
cheek /tʃiːk/ **32**
cheese /tʃiːz/ **57**
cheeseburger /'tʃiːzbɜːgər/ **61**
cheesecake /'tʃiːzkeɪk/ **60**
cheese on toast /ˌ.. . '. / **64**
cheetah /'tʃiːtə/ **96**
chef /ʃef/ **21**
chemistry /'kemɪstri/ **53**
chemist's /'kemɪsts/ **78**
cheque /tʃek/ **73**
chequebook /'tʃekbʊk/ **73**
cheque card /'tʃek kɑːd/ **73**
cherry /'tʃeri/ **56**
chess /tʃes/ **89**
chest /tʃest/ **31**
chestnut tree /'tʃesnʌt triː/ **106**
chest of drawers /ˌ.. . '. / **11**
chewing gum /'tʃuːɪŋ gʌm/ **77**
Chicago /ʃɪ'kɑːgəʊ/ **105**
chick /tʃɪk/ **95**
chicken /'tʃɪkɪn/ **95**
chicken curry with rice /ˌtʃɪkɪn ˌkʌri wɪð 'raɪs/ **64**
chicken leg /'tʃɪkɪn leg/ **59**
chicken liver pâté /ˌtʃɪkɪn ˌlɪvə 'pæteɪ/ **60**
child /tʃaɪld/ **4, 5, 51**
children /'tʃɪldrən/ **5**

chilly /'tʃɪli/ **107**
chimney /'tʃɪmni/ **7**
chin /tʃɪn/ **31**
chips /tʃɪps/ **57, 61**
chiropodist /kɪ'rɒpədɪst/ **40**
chisel /'tʃɪzəl/ **26**
chocolate gateau
/,tʃɒklɪt 'gætəʊ/ **60**
chop /tʃɒp/ **63**
chopped tomatoes
/,tʃɒpt tə'mɑːtəʊz‖-'meɪ-/
57
chopping board /'tʃɒpɪŋ bɔːd/
8
chorus /'kɔːrəs/ **87**
Christmas Day /,krɪsməs 'deɪ/
102
chrysanthemum
/krɪ'sænθɪməm/ **16**
church /tʃɜːtʃ/ **93**
cinema /'sɪnɪmə/ **87**
circle /'sɜːkəl/ **101**
circumference /sə'kʌmfərəns/
101
city wall /sɪti 'wɔːl/ **93**
clam /klæm/ **97**
clap /klæp/ **34**
clarinet /,klærɪ'net/ **90**
classical concert
/,klæsɪkəl 'kɒnsət/ **87**
classifieds /'klæsɪfaɪdz/ **20**
claw /klɔː/ **97**
claws /klɔːz/ **98**
cleaning fluid /'kliːnɪŋ ,fluːɪd/
42
clear /klɪər/ **107**
clementine /'kleməntiːn/ **56**
cliff /klɪf/ **106**
climber /'klaɪmər/ **83**
climbing /'klaɪmɪŋ/ **83**
climbing frame
/'klaɪmɪŋ freɪm/ **51**
clingfilm™ /'klɪŋfɪlm/ **8**
clock /klɒk/ **65, 103**
clock radio /klɒk 'reɪdiəʊ/ **111**
close /kləʊz/ **114**
closed /kləʊzd/ **114**
clothes line /'kləʊðz laɪn/ **15**
cloudy /'klaʊdi/ **107**
clutch /klʌtʃ/ **67**
clutch bag /'klʌtʃ bæg/ **49**
coach /kəʊtʃ/ **65**
coaster /'kəʊstər/ **13**
coastline /'kəʊstlaɪn/ **106**
coat /kəʊt/ **43**
coat hanger /'kəʊt ,hæŋər/ **15**
cockatoo /,kɒkə'tuː/ **98**
cockerel /'kɒkərəl/ **95**
cockpit /'kɒk,pɪt/ **71**
cockroach /'kɒk-rəʊtʃ/ **99**
cocoa /'kəʊkəʊ/ **58**
coconut /'kəʊkənʌt/ **56**
cod fillet /kɒd 'fɪlɪt/ **59**
coffee /'kɒfi/ **58, 60, 64**
coffee maker /'kɒfi ,meɪkər/ **9**
coffee table /'.. ,../ **12**
coin /kɔɪn/ **88**
coin album /'kɔɪn ,ælbəm/ **88**
coin collecting /'kɔɪn kə,lektɪŋ/
88
cola /'kəʊlə/ **58, 61**

cold /kəʊld/ **107**
cold /kəʊld/ **38, 39**
cold remedy /'kəʊld ,remɪdi/
39
cold water tap /. '.. ./ **10**
coleslaw /'kəʊlslɔː/ **59**
collar /'kɒlər/ **46**
collection /kə'lekʃən/ **76**
cologne /kə'ləʊn/ **37**
Colorado /,kɒlə'rɑːdəʊ/ **105**
coloured pen /,kʌləd 'pen/ **77**
colour film /'kʌlə fɪlm/ **77**
colouring book /'kʌlərɪŋ bʊk/
51, 77
colours /'kʌləz/ **47**
comb /kəʊm/ **36, 37**
comb your hair /,. . './ **6**
comet /'kɒmɪt/ **108**
compact disc/CD player
/,kɒmpækt 'dɪsk pleɪər, siː
'diː ,pleɪər/ **111**
compass /'kʌmpəs/ **52**
compost
/'kɒmpɒst‖'kɑːmpəʊst/ **17**
computer /kəm'pjuːtər/ **52**
computer games /.'.. ,./ **89,
109**
computer techician
/kəm'pjuːtə tek,nɪʃən/ **23**
condiments /'kɒndɪmənts/ **58**
conditioner /kən'dɪʃənər/ **10,
37**
conductor /kən'dʌktər/ **87**
cone /kəʊn/ **61**
confectionery /kən'fekʃənəri/
77
conference room
/'kɒnfərəns ruːm/ **29**
confused /kən'fjuːzd/ **113**
conkers /'kɒŋkəz/ **106**
Connecticut /kə'netɪkət/ **105**
console /'kɒnsəʊl/ **109**
constellation /,kɒnstə'leɪʃən/
108
construction worker
/kən'strʌkʃən ,wɜːkər/ **28**
consultant /kən'sʌltənt/ **41**
contact lens /'kɒntækt lenz/
42
container /kən'teɪnər/ **62**
control tower
/kən'trəʊl ,taʊər/ **71**
convertible /kən'vɜːtəbəl/ **66**
conveyor belt /kən'veɪə belt/
27, 57
cook /kʊk/ **19, 21, 63**
cookery /'kʊkəri/ **88**
cookery book /'... ./ **8**
cooking pot /'kʊkɪŋ pɒt/ **8**
cool /kuːl/ **107**
co-pilot /'kəʊ,paɪlət/ **71**
cordless phone /,kɔːdləs 'fəʊn/
112
Cork /kɔːk/ **104**
corned beef /,kɔːnd 'biːf/ **57**
corner /'kɔːnər/ **101**
corn on the cob
/,kɔːn ɒn ðə 'kɒb/ **55**
correction fluid
/kə'rekʃən ,fluːɪd/ **24, 77**
cosmetics /kɒz'metɪks/ **36**

cot /kɒt/ **14**
cottage /'kɒtɪdʒ/ **7**
cotton /'kɒtn/ **48**
couch /kaʊtʃ/ **36**
cough /kɒf/ **38, 39**
cough mixture /'kɒf ,mɪkstʃər/
39
counsellor /'kaʊnsələr/ **40**
counter /'kaʊntər/ **73, 76**
country code /'kʌntri kəʊd/
79
country of birth
/,kʌntri əv 'bɜːθ/ **4**
courgette /kʊə'ʒet/ **55**
court /kɔːt/ **82**
court reporter /,kɔːt rɪ'pɔːtər/
30
courtroom /'kɔːtrʊm/ **30**
court shoes /'kɔːt ʃuːz/ **43**
cousin /'kʌzən/ **5**
covering letter /,kʌvərɪŋ 'letər/
20
cow /kaʊ/ **95**
crab /kræb/ **59, 97**
cracked lips /krækt 'lɪps/ **39**
craft fair /'krɑːft feər/ **93**
crafts /krɑːfts/ **88**
crane /kreɪn/ **28, 72, 98**
crayons /'kreɪɒnz/ **51**
cream /kriːm/ **39, 47, 57, 60**
credit card /'kredɪt kɑːd/ **73**
crest /krest/ **95**
crewneck jumper
/,kruːnek 'dʒʌmpər/ **43**
cricket /'krɪkɪt/ **80**
cricket ball /'.. ./ **80**
cricket pitch /'.. ./ **80**
crisps /krɪsps/ **61**
crockery /'krɒkəri/ **13**
crocodile /'krɒkədaɪl/ **96**
croissant /'kwɑːsɒŋ/ **64**
cropped hair /,krɒpt 'heər/ **33**
cross-country skiing
/,krɒs kʌntri 'skiːɪŋ/ **85**
crossroads /'krɒsrəʊdz/ **68**
crow /krəʊ/ **98**
crowd /kraʊd/ **80**
cruise ship /'kruːz ʃɪp/ **72**
crush /krʌʃ/ **63**
crutch /krʌtʃ/ **41**
cry /kraɪ/ **34**
cube /kjuːb/ **101**
cucumber /'kjuːkʌmbər/ **55**
cuff /kʌf/ **46**
cuff link /'kʌf lɪŋk/ **49**
cup /kʌp/ **13**
cupboard /'kʌbəd/ **8**
cupful /'kʌpfʊl/ **62**
curly hair /,kɜːli 'heər/ **33**
cursor /'kɜːsər/ **109**
curtain /'kɜːtn/ **12**
cushion /'kʊʃən/ **12**
customer /'kʌstəmər/ **57, 73**
customs /'kʌstəmz/ **70**
customs officer
/'kʌstəmz ,ɒfɪsər/ **70**
cut /kʌt/ **35, 36**
cut /kʌt/ **38, 39**
cutlery /'kʌtləri/ **13**
cut up /kʌt 'ʌp/ **63**
CV /,siː 'viː/ **20**

cycling /'saɪklɪŋ/ **83**
cyclist /'saɪklɪst/ **83**
cyclists only sign
/,saɪklɪsts 'əʊnli saɪn/ **69**
cylinder /'sɪlɪndər/ **101**
cylinder block /'sɪlɪndə blɒk/
66
cymbal /'sɪmbəl/ **90**

daffodil /'dæfədɪl/ **16**
dairy products
/'deəri ,prɒdʌkts/ **57**
daisy /'deɪzi/ **16**
Dallas /'dæləs/ **105**
dam /dæm/ **106**
dance /dɑːns/ **34**
dark /dɑːk/ **114**
dark hair /,dɑːk 'heər/ **33**
dashboard /'dæʃbɔːd/ **67**
date /deɪt/ **56**
date of birth /,deɪt əv 'bɜːθ/ **4**
daughter /'dɔːtər/ **5**
daughter-in-law /'dɔːtər ɪn lɔː/
5
day school /'deɪ skuːl/ **50**
days of the week
/,deɪz əv ðə 'wiːk/ **102**
debit card /'debɪt kɑːd/ **73**
decay /dɪ'keɪ/ **42**
December /dɪ'sembər/ **102**
deck /dek/ **72**
deckchair /'dektʃeər/ **91**
deep /diːp/ **114**
deer /dɪər/ **96**
defendant /dɪ'fendənt/ **30**
defender /dɪ'fendər/ **80**
degrees Celsius/degrees
Centigrade /dɪ,griːz 'selsiəs,
dɪ,griːz 'sentɪgreɪd/ **107**
degrees Fahrenheit
/dɪ,griːz 'færənhaɪt/ **107**
Delaware /'deləweər/ **105**
delicatessen /,delɪkə'tesən/ **59**
delivery /dɪ'lɪvəri/ **76**
denim /'denɪm/ **48**
dental floss /'dentl flɒs/ **42**
dental nurse /'dentl nɜːs/ **42**
dentist /'dentɪst/ **22, 42**
dentures /'dentʃəz/ **42**
Denver /'denvər/ **105**
department store
/dɪ'pɑːtmənt ,stɔːr/ **74, 78**
departure gates /dɪ'pɑːtʃə
,geɪts/ **70**
deposit box/slot /dɪ'pɒzɪt
,bɒks, dɪ'pɒzɪt ,slɒt/ **73**
depth /depθ/ **101**
dermatologist
/,dɜːmə'tɒlədʒɪst/ **40**
desert /'dezət/ **106**
design and technology
/dɪ,zaɪn ən tek'nɒlədʒi/ **53**
designer /dɪ'zaɪnər/ **23**
desk /desk/ **24, 52**
desk diary /'desk ,daɪəri/ **24**
desk lamp /'desk læmp/ **24**
desk tidy /'desk ,taɪdi/ **24**
desserts /dɪ'zɜːts/ **60**
dessertspoon /dɪ'zɜːtspuːn/ **13**
dessert trolley /dɪ'zɜːt ,trɒli/
60

WORDLIST

detached house /dɪˌtætʃt 'haʊs/ 7
diagonal /daɪ'æɡənəl/ 101
dialling code /'daɪəlɪŋ kəʊd/ 79
diameter /daɪ'æmɪtər/ 101
diamond /'daɪəmənd/ 49
dice /daɪs/ 89
dictionary /'dɪkʃənəri/ 54
dietician /ˌdaɪə'tɪʃən/ 40
digger /'dɪɡər/ 28
digital camera /ˌdɪdʒɪtl 'kæmərə/ 112
digital watch /ˌdɪdʒɪtl 'wɒtʃ/ 103
dig the soil /ˌdɪɡ ðə 'sɔɪl/ 17
dining room /'daɪnɪŋ ruːm/ 18
dining room table /ˌ... '../ 13
dinner /'dɪnər/ 64
dinner jacket /'.. ˌ../ 45
dishcloth /'dɪʃklɒθ/ 8
dishwasher /'dɪʃˌwɒʃər/ 8
display screen /dɪ'spleɪ skriːn/ 109
distributor /dɪ'strɪbjʊtər/ 66
diver /'daɪvər/ 84
diving /'daɪvɪŋ/ 84
diving board /'.. ./ 84
divorced /dɪ'vɔːst/ 4
DIY /ˌdiː aɪ 'waɪ/ 88
do a handstand /duː ə 'hændstænd/ 86
dock /dɒk/ 72
doctor /'dɒktər/ 22, 40
Doctor of Philosophy (PhD) /ˌdɒktər əv fɪ'lɒsəfi, ˌpiː eɪtʃ 'diː/ 50
Doctor's Surgery /ˌdɒktəz 'sɜːdʒəri/ 40
document /'dɒkjʊmənt/ 109
document case /'dɒkjʊmənt ˌkeɪs/ 49
dog /dɒɡ/ 94
dog food /'dɒɡ fuːd/ 58
do homework /duː 'həʊmwɜːk/ 19
doll /dɒl/ 51
doll's pram /'dɒlz præm/ 51
dolphin /'dɒlfɪn/ 97
donkey /'dɒŋki/ 95
door /dɔːr/ 67
doorbell /'dɔːbel/ 7
door handle /'. ../ 8
doorknob /'dɔːnɒb/ 7
doorstep /'dɔːstep/ 7
do press-ups /duː 'pres ʌps/ 86
dormitory /'dɔːmɪtəri/ 50
do sit-ups /duː 'sɪt ʌps/ 86
do the laundry /duː ðə 'lɔːndri/ 19
double bass /ˌdʌbəl 'beɪs/ 90
double bed /ˌdʌbəl 'bed/ 11
double room /ˌdʌbəl ruːm/ 29
double yellow line /ˌdʌbəl jeləʊ 'laɪn/ 74
doughnut /'dəʊnʌt/ 61
Dover /'dəʊvər/ 104
down /daʊn/ 115
downhill skiing /ˌdaʊnhɪl 'skiːɪŋ/ 85
downstairs /ˌdaʊn'steəz/ 18

dragonfly /'dræɡənflaɪ/ 99
drainpipe /'dreɪnpaɪp/ 7
drama /'drɑːmə/ 53
drape AmE /dreɪp/ 12
draughts /drɑːfts/ 89
draughtsman /'drɑːftsmən/ 23
draw /drɔː/ 35
drawer /drɔːr/ 8, 11
drawing pins /'drɔːɪŋ pɪnz/ 77
dress /dres/ 44
dressing gown /'dresɪŋ ɡaʊn/ 43
dressing table /'dresɪŋ ˌteɪbəl/ 11
dressmaker /'dres,meɪkər/ 48
drill /drɪl/ 42
drill bits /'drɪl bɪts/ 26
drinks /drɪŋks/ 58, 60
drip /drɪp/ 79
drive /draɪv/ 7
drum /drʌm/ 90
drum kit /'drʌm kɪt/ 90
dry /draɪ/ 114
dry goods /'draɪ ɡʊdz/ 58
dry yourself /'draɪ jəself/ 6
dual carriageway /ˌdjuːəl 'kærɪdʒweɪ/ 68
Dublin /'dʌblɪn/ 104
duck /dʌk/ 95
duckling /'dʌklɪŋ/ 95
dummy /'dʌmi/ 14
dumper truck /'dʌmpə trʌk/ 28
Dun Laoghaire /dʌn 'lɪəri/ 104
Dundee /dʌn'diː/ 104
dungarees /ˌdʌŋɡə'riːz/ 44, 51
Durham /'dʌrəm/ 104
dust /dʌst/ 19
duster /'dʌstər/ 19
dustpan /'dʌstpæn/ 15
duty free shop /ˌdjuːti 'friː ʃɒp/ 70
duvet /'duːveɪ, 'djuː-/ 11
DVD /ˌdiː viː 'diː/ 111
DVD player /ˌ. .'. ˌ../ 111

eagle /'iːɡəl/ 98
ear /ɪər/ 31
ear, nose and throat specialist /ˌɪə nəʊz ən 'θrəʊt ˌspeʃəlɪst/ 40
ear protectors/defenders /'ɪə prəˌtektəz, 'ɪə dɪˌfendəz/ 28
earring /'ɪərɪŋ/ 49
Earth /ɜːθ/ 108
easel /'iːzəl/ 51
Easter Day /'iːstə deɪ/ 102
eat breakfast /iːt 'brekfəst/ 6
ecstatic /ɪk'stætɪk/ 113
edge /edʒ/ 101
Edinburgh /'edɪnbərə/ 104
eel /iːl/ 97
egg /eɡ/ 57, 98
eight /eɪt/ 100
eight am/eight (o'clock) in the morning /ˌeɪt eɪ 'em, ˌeɪt əklɒk ɪn ðə 'mɔːnɪŋ/ 103
eighteen /ˌeɪ'tiːn/ 100

eighteen hundred hours /ˌeɪtiːn 'hʌndrəd aʊəz/ 103
eight pm/eight (o'clock) in the evening /ˌeɪt piː 'em, ˌeɪt əklɒk ɪn ði 'iːvnɪŋ/ 103
eighty /'eɪti/ 100
elastic band /ɪˌlæstɪk 'bænd/ 24
elbow /'elbəʊ/ 31
elderly /'eldəli/ 4
electric blanket /ɪˌlektrɪk 'blæŋkɪt/ 11
electric drill /ɪˌlektrɪk 'drɪl/ 26
electric guitar /ɪˌlektrɪk ɡɪ'tɑːr/ 90
electrician /ɪˌlek'trɪʃən, ˌelɪk-/ 21
electric mixer /ɪˌlektrɪk 'mɪksər/ 9
electric shaver /ɪˌlektrɪk 'ʃeɪvər/ 37
electric typewriter /ɪˌlektrɪk 'taɪpˌraɪtər/ 24, 111
electric window button /ɪˌlektrɪk 'wɪndəʊ ˌbʌtn/ 67
electronic games /ˌelɪktrɒnɪk 'ɡeɪmz/ 109
electronic personal organiser /ˌelɪktrɒnɪk ˌpɜːsənəl 'ɔːɡənaɪzər/ 112
electronics shop /ɪˌlek'trɒnɪks ʃɒp/ 78
elephant /'elɪfənt/ 96
elevator AmE /'eləveɪtər/ 29
eleven /ɪ'levən/ 100
eleven hundred hours /ɪˌlevən 'hʌndrəd aʊəz/ 103
e-mail /'iː meɪl/ 20, 110
e-mail address /'iː meɪl əˌdres‖-ˌædres/ 4, 110
embroidery /ɪm'brɔɪdəri/ 88
emerald /'emərəld/ 49
emergency number /ɪ'mɜːdʒənsi ˌnʌmbər/ 79
emery board /'eməri bɔːd/ 37
empty /'empti/ 62, 114
encyclopedia /ɪnˌsaɪklə'piːdiə/ 54
engine /'endʒɪn/ 65, 66
England /'ɪŋɡlənd/ 104
English /'ɪŋɡlɪʃ/ 53
en suite shower room /ɒn swiːt 'ʃaʊə ruːm/ 18
envelope /'envələʊp/ 76
escalator /'eskəleɪtər/ 78
estate agent /ɪ'steɪt ˌeɪdʒənt/ 23
estate car /ɪ'steɪt kɑːr/ 66
evening gown /'iːvnɪŋ ɡaʊn/ 44
evidence /'evɪdəns/ 30
examination couch /ɪɡˌzæmɪ'neɪʃən kaʊtʃ/ 40
excavation site /ˌekskə'veɪʃən saɪt/ 28
excavator /'ekskəveɪtər/ 28
exchange rates /ɪks'tʃeɪndʒ reɪts/ 73
exercise bike /'eksəsaɪz baɪk/ 86

exercise book /'eksəsaɪz bʊk/ 52
exhaust pipe /ɪɡ'zɔːst paɪp/ 67
exhibition /ˌeksɪ'bɪʃən/ 93
ex-husband /ˌeks 'hʌzbənd/ 5
expensive /ɪk'spensɪv/ 114
ex-wife /ˌeks 'waɪf/ 5
eye /aɪ/ 31
eyebrow /'aɪbraʊ/ 32
eyebrow pencil /'.. ˌ../ 37
eye drops /'aɪ drɒps/ 39, 42
eyelash /'aɪlæʃ/ 32
eyelid /'aɪlɪd/ 32
eyeliner /'aɪˌlaɪnər/ 37
eye shadow /'aɪ ˌʃædəʊ/ 37

fabric conditioner /'fæbrɪk kənˌdɪʃənər/ 15
fabric shop /'fæbrɪk ʃɒp/ 78
face /feɪs/ 31, 101, 103
facecloth /'feɪsklɒθ/ 10
facial /'feɪʃəl/ 36
factory worker /'fæktəri ˌwɜːkər/ 23
fair hair /ˌfeə 'heər/ 33
falcon /'fɔːlkən/ 98
fall /fɔːl/ 34, 86
fall AmE /fɔːl/ 107
family name /'fæməli neɪm/ 4
fans /fænz/ 80
far /fɑːr/ 114
farmer /'fɑːmər/ 21
fast /fɑːst/ 114
father /'fɑːðər/ 5
father-in-law /'fɑːðər ɪn lɔː/ 5
Father's Day /'fɑːðəz deɪ/ 102
fatty tissue /ˌfæti 'tɪʃuː/ 32
faucet AmE /'fɔːsɪt/ 8
fax a document /ˌfæks ə 'dɒkjʊmənt/ 25
fax machine /'fæks məˌʃiːn/ 24
fax number /'fæks ˌnʌmbər/ 20
feather /'feðər/ 98
February /'februəri/ 102
feed /fiːd/ 19
feelings /'fiːlɪŋz/ 113
fence /fens/ 7, 17
ferry /'feri/ 72
fertiliser /'fɜːtɪlaɪzər/ 17
festivals /'festɪvəlz/ 102
field /fiːld/ 106
fielder /'fiːldər/ 80
fifteen /ˌfɪf'tiːn/ 100
fifteen hundred hours /ˌfɪftiːn 'hʌndrəd ˌaʊəz/ 103
fifth /fɪfθ/ 100
fifty /'fɪfti/ 100
fifty pence/fifty pence piece /ˌfɪfti 'pens, ˌfɪfti pens 'piːs/ 73
fifty percent /ˌfɪfti pə'sent/ 100
fifty pounds/fifty pound note /ˌfɪfti 'paʊndz, ˌfɪfti paʊnd 'nəʊt/ 73
fig /fɪɡ/ 56
figure skate /'fɪɡə skeɪt/ 85
figure skater /'fɪɡə ˌskeɪtər/ 85

figure skating /'fɪgə ˌskeɪtɪŋ/ **85**
file /faɪl/ **24, 26, 109**
file papers /ˌfaɪl 'peɪpəz/ **25**
filing cabinet /'faɪlɪŋ ˌkæbɪnət/ **25**
fill /fɪl/ **35**
fill in a form /ˌfɪl ɪn ə 'fɔːm/ **25**
filling /'fɪlɪŋ/ **42**
film /fɪlm/ **87, 112**
Filofax™ /'faɪləʊˌfæks/ **49**
fin /fɪn/ **97**
financial advisor /fə'nænʃəl əd'vaɪzər/ **23**
finger /'fɪŋgər/ **31**
fir cone /'fɜː kəʊn/ **106**
fire /faɪər/ **79**
fire brigade /'faɪə brɪˌgeɪd/ **79**
fire engine /'. ˌ../ **79**
fire extinguisher /'faɪər ɪkˌstɪŋwɪʃər/ **27, 79**
fire fighter /'faɪə ˌfaɪtər/ **22, 79**
fireguard /'faɪəgɑːd/ **12**
fireplace /'faɪəpleɪs/ **12**
first /fɜːst/ **100**
first-aid kit /ˌfɜːst 'eɪd kɪt/ **27**
first class /ˌfɜːst 'klɑːs/ **65**
first class post /ˌfɜːst klɑːs 'pəʊst/ **76**
first floor /ˌ. './ **18**
first name /'. ./ **4**
first school /'fɜːst skuːl/ **50**
fir tree /'fɜː triː/ **106**
fish /fɪʃ/ **97**
fish and chips /ˌfɪʃ ən 'tʃɪps/ **61**
fish and seafood /fɪʃ ən 'siːfuːd/
fisherman /'fɪʃəmən/ **21, 84**
fish fingers /ˌfɪʃ 'fɪŋgəz/ **57**
fish fingers with mashed potatoes /fɪʃ ˌfɪŋgəz wɪð ˌmæʃt pə'teɪtəʊz/ **64**
fishing /'fɪʃɪŋ/ **84**
fishing hook /'.. ../ **92**
fishing line /'fɪʃɪŋ laɪn/ **84**
fishing rod /'fɪʃɪŋ rɒd/ **84, 92**
fish tank /'fɪʃ tæŋk/ **94**
fitted sheet /ˌfɪtɪd 'ʃiːt/ **11**
five /faɪv/ **100**
five pence/five pence piece /ˌfaɪv 'pens, ˌfaɪv pens 'piːs/ **73**
five pounds/five pound note /ˌfaɪv 'paʊndz, ˌfaɪv paʊnd 'nəʊt/ **73**
fizzy drink /'fɪzi drɪŋk/ **61**
fizzy mineral water /ˌfɪzi 'mɪnərəl ˌwɔːtər/ **60**
flag /flæg/ **75, 108**
flamingo /flə'mɪŋgəʊ/ **98**
flannel /'flænl/ **10**
flash /flæʃ/ **112**
flats /flæts/ **7**
fleece /fliːs/ **43**
flight information screen /ˌflaɪt ɪnfə'meɪʃən ˌskriːn/ **70**
flipper /'flɪpər/ **97, 98**

floor /flɔːr/ **18**
floppy disk/diskette /ˌflɒpi 'dɪsk, dɪ'sket/ **109**
Florida /'flɒrɪdə/ **105**
florist /'flɒrɪst/ **21**
flour /flaʊər/ **58**
flowerbed /'flaʊəbed/ **16**
flowers /'flaʊəz/ **12, 16**
flu /fluː/ **38**
flute /fluːt/ **90**
fly /flaɪ/ **99**
flyover /'flaɪ-əʊvər/ **68**
foal /fəʊl/ **95**
foggy /'fɒgi/ **107**
fold /fəʊld/ **35**
folder /'fəʊldər/ **109**
font /fɒnt/ **109**
food processor /'fuːd ˌprəʊsesər/ **9**
foot /fʊt/ **31**
football /'fʊtbɔːl/ **80**
football boots /'.. ../ **80**
footballer /'fʊtbɔːlər/ **80**
footrest /'fʊt-rest/ **36**
footwear /'fʊtweər/ **43**
forearm /'fɔːrɑːm/ **31**
forehead /'fɒrɪd, 'fɔːhed/ **32**
foreign currency /ˌfɒrɪn 'kʌrənsi/ **73**
foreman /'fɔːmən/ **27**
forest /'fɒrɪst/ **106**
fork /fɔːk/ **13, 17**
forklift /'fɔːklɪft/ **27**
formal wear /'fɔːməl weər/ **44, 45**
forth /fɔːθ/ **100**
forty /'fɔːti/ **100**
foundation /faʊn'deɪʃən/ **37**
four /fɔːr/ **100**
four (degrees) below (zero)/minus twenty (degrees) /ˌfɔː ˌdɪˌgriːz bɪləʊ 'zɪərəʊ, ˌmaɪnəs ˌtwenti dɪ'griːz/ **107**
fourteen /ˌfɔː'tiːn/ **100**
four-wheel drive /ˌfɔː wiːl 'draɪv/ **66**
fox /fɒks/ **96**
foyer /'fɔɪeɪ/ **29**
frame /freɪm/ **42**
franking machine /'fræŋkɪŋ məˌʃiːn/ **24**
freezer /'friːzər/ **8**
freezing /'friːzɪŋ/ **107**
freight elevator /'freɪt ˌeləveɪtər/ **27**
French /frentʃ/ **53**
French bean /ˌfrentʃ 'biːn/ **55**
French fries /ˌfrentʃ 'fraɪz/ **61**
French horn /ˌfrentʃ 'hɔːn/ **90**
Friday /'fraɪdi/ **102**
fridge /frɪdʒ/ **8**
fried chicken /ˌfraɪd 'tʃɪkɪn/ **61**
fringe /frɪndʒ/ **33**
frog /frɒg/ **96**
from /frɒm/ **115**
front door /ˌfrʌnt 'dɔːr/ **7**
front garden /ˌfrʌnt 'gɑːdn/ **7**
front teeth /ˌfrʌnt 'tiːθ/ **42**
frown /fraʊn/ **34**

frozen foods /ˌfrəʊzən 'fuːdz/ **57**
fry /fraɪ/ **63**
frying pan /'fraɪ-ɪŋ pæn/ **9**
fudge /fʌdʒ/ **77**
fuel gauge /'fjuːəl geɪdʒ/ **67**
fuel tank /'fjuːəl tæŋk/ **108**
full /fʊl/ **62, 114**
full cream milk /ˌfʊl kriːm 'mɪlk/ **64**
full moon /fʊl 'muːn/ **108**
fur /fɜːr/ **94**
furious /'fjʊəriəs/ **113**
further education college /ˌfɜːðər edjʊ'keɪʃən ˌkɒlɪdʒ/ **50**

galaxy /'gæləksi/ **108**
Galway /'gɔːlweɪ/ **104**
games /geɪmz/ **89**
games console /. ˌ../ **111**
garage /'gærɑːʒ‖gə'rɑːʒ/ **7, 66**
gardener /'gɑːdnər/ **21**
garden gloves /'gɑːdn glʌvz/ **17**
gardening /'gɑːdnɪŋ/ **88**
garden shed /ˌgɑːdn 'ʃed/ **16**
garlic /'gɑːlɪk/ **55**
garlic press /'.. ../ **9**
gate /geɪt/ **7, 81**
gateau /'gætəʊ/ **60**
gauze pad /'gɔːz pæd/ **39**
GCSE/Standard Grade /ˌdʒiː siː es 'iː, 'stændəd ˌgreɪd/ **50**
gear lever/stick /'gɪə ˌliːvər, 'gɪə stɪk/ **67**
gear shift AmE /'gɪə ʃɪft/ **67**
gems /dʒemz/ **49**
general practitioner (GP) /ˌdʒenərəl præk'tɪʃənər, ˌdʒiː 'piː/ **40**
general view /'dʒenərəl vjuː/ **60**
geography /dʒi'ɒgrəfi/ **53**
Georgia /'dʒɔːdʒə/ **105**
geranium /dʒə'reɪniəm/ **16**
gerbil /'dʒɜːbəl/ **94**
German /'dʒɜːmən/ **53**
get dressed /get 'drest/ **6**
get up /get 'ʌp/ **6**
gherkins /'gɜːkɪnz/ **61**
gills /gɪlz/ **97**
ginger hair /ˌdʒɪndʒə 'heər/ **33**
giraffe /dʒɪ'rɑːf/ **96**
girder /'gɜːdər/ **28**
girl /gɜːl/ **4**
give /gɪv/ **35**
give way sign /gɪv 'weɪ saɪn/ **69**
Glasgow /'glæzgəʊ/ **104**
glasses /'glɑːsɪz/ **42**
glasses case /'glɑːsɪz keɪs/ **42**
glove /glʌv/ **81**
gloves /glʌvz/ **43**
glue /gluː/ **35, 51**
GNVQ /ˌdʒiː en viː 'kjuː/ **50**
goal /gəʊl/ **80**
goal area /'gəʊl ˌeəriə/ **80**
goalie /'gəʊli/ **80**
goal line /'gəʊl laɪn/ **80**
goalkeeper /'gəʊlˌkiːpər/ **80**

goalpost /'gəʊlpəʊst/ **80**
goatee /gəʊ'tiː/ **33**
goggles /'gɒgəlz/ **52, 84**
gold /gəʊld/ **49**
goldfish /'gəʊldˌfɪʃ/ **94**
goldfish bowl /'.. ../ **94**
golf /gɒlf/ **83**
golf ball /'. ./ **83**
golf club /'gɒlf klʌb/ **83**
golfer /'gɒlfər/ **83**
goose /guːs/ **95**
gooseberry /'gʊzbəri/ **56**
gorilla /gə'rɪlə/ **96**
go shopping /gəʊ 'ʃɒpɪŋ/ **19**
gosling /'gɒzlɪŋ/ **95**
go to bed /ˌgəʊ tə 'bed/ **6**
go to work /ˌgəʊ tə 'wɜːk/ **6**
gown /gaʊn/ **36**
grams /græmz/ **62**
grandchildren /'grænˌtʃɪldrən/ **5**
granddaughter /'grænˌdɔːtər/ **5**
grandfather /'grænˌfɑːðər/ **5**
grandmother /'grænˌmʌðər/ **5**
grandparents /'grænˌpeərənts/ **5**
grandson /'grænsʌn/ **5**
grape /greɪp/ **56**
grapefruit /'greɪpfruːt/ **56, 64**
grass /grɑːs/ **106**
grasshopper /'grɑːsˌhɒpər/ **99**
grate /greɪt/ **63**
grater /'greɪtər/ **9**
graze /greɪz/ **38, 39**
grease /griːs/ **63**
Great Salt Lake /ˌgreɪt sɔːlt 'leɪk/ **105**
green /griːn/ **47, 68, 83**
greengrocer /'griːnˌgrəʊsər/ **21**
greenhouse /'griːnhaʊs/ **16**
green pepper /ˌ. '../ **55**
greet visitors /ˌgriːt 'vɪzɪtəz/ **25**
grey /greɪ/ **47**
grill /grɪl/ **63**
ground floor /ˌgraʊnd 'flɔːr/ **18**
groundsheet /'graʊndʃiːt/ **92**
guard /gɑːd/ **30**
guest /gest/ **29**
guinea pig /'gɪni pɪg/ **94**
Gulf of Mexico /ˌgʌlf əv 'meksɪkəʊ/ **105**
gull /gʌl/ **98**
gum /gʌm/ **42**
gutter /'gʌtər/ **7, 74**
Guy Fawkes Night /gaɪ 'fɔːks naɪt/ **102**
gymnast /'dʒɪmnæst/ **83**
gymnastics /dʒɪm'næstɪks/ **83**
gynaecologist /ˌgaɪnə'kɒlədʒɪst/ **40**

hack saw /'hæk sɔː/ **26**
hair /heər/ **31**
hairbrush /'heəbrʌʃ/ **36, 37**
hair colour /'heə ˌkʌlər/ **36**
hairdresser /'heəˌdresər/ **23, 36**
hairdryer /'heəˌdraɪər/ **36, 37**
hair slide /'heə slaɪd/ **49**

hairspray /'heəspreɪ/ **36**
hair wax /'heə wæks/ **36**
half-brother /'hɑːf brʌðər/ **5**
half moon /ˌhɑːf 'muːn/ **108**
half-sister /'hɑːf sɪstər/ **5**
halfway line /ˌhɑːf'weɪ laɪn/ **80**
Halloween /ˌhæləʊ'iːn/ **102**
hallway /'hɔːlweɪ/ **18**
ham /hæm/ **59**
hamburger /'hæmbɜːgər/ **61**
hammer /'hæmər/ **26**
ham salad /hæm 'sæləd/ **64**
hamster /'hæmstər/ **94**
hand /hænd/ **31**
hand beater /'hænd ˌbiːtər/ **9**
handbag /'hændbæg/ **49**
handcuffs /'hændkʌfs/ **30**
handkerchief /'hæŋkətʃɪf/ **49**
handle /'hændl/ **9, 11**
hand luggage /'hænd ˌlʌgɪdʒ/ **70**
hand mirror /'hænd ˌmɪrər/ **36**
hand saw /'hænd sɔː/ **26**
hand towel /'hænd ˌtaʊəl/ **10**
hand truck /'hænd trʌk/ **27**
hangar /'hæŋər/ **71**
hang glider /'hæŋ ˌglaɪdər/ **83**
hang gliding /'hæŋ ˌglaɪdɪŋ/ **83**
happy /'hæpi/ **113**
hard /hɑːd/ **114**
hard disk drive /hɑːd 'dɪsk draɪv/ **109**
hard hat /'. ./ **28**
hard shoulder /. '../ **68**
hardware /'hɑːdweər/ **109**
harmonica /hɑː'mɒnɪkə/ **90**
harness /'hɑːnɪs/ **83**
hat /hæt/ **43**
hatchback /'hætʃbæk/ **66**
hatchet /'hætʃɪt/ **26**
have a bath /hæv ə 'bɑːθ/ **6**
have a cup of coffee /hæv ə ˌkʌp əv 'kɒfi/ **6**
have a shower /hæv ə 'ʃaʊər/ **6**
Hawaii /hə'waɪ-i/ **105**
hayfever /'heɪˌfiːvər/ **39**
hazelnut /'heɪzəlnʌt/ **56**
hazy /'heɪzi/ **107**
head /hed/ **31**
headache /'hedeɪk/ **38, 39**
headboard /'hedbɔːd/ **11**
headlight /'hedlaɪt/ **67**
headphones /'hedfəʊnz/ **111**
headrest /'hed-rest/ **67**
heart /hɑːt/ **32**
heat control /'hiːt kənˌtrəʊl/ **11**
heavy /'hevi/ **114**
hedge /hedʒ/ **16**
hedgehog /'hedʒhɒg/ **99**
hedge trimmer /'hedʒ ˌtrɪmər/ **17**
heel /hiːl/ **31, 46**
height /haɪt/ **101**
height-adjustable chair /ˌhaɪt ədʒʌstəbəl 'tʃeər/ **36**
height chart /'haɪt tʃɑːt/ **40**
helicopter /'helɪkɒptər/ **71**

helmet /'helmɪt/ **80, 83, 85**
hemline /'hemlaɪn/ **46**
herbal tea /ˌhɜːbəl 'tiː/ **58**
hi-fi /'haɪ faɪ/ **111**
high chair /'haɪ tʃeər/ **14**
highlights /'haɪlaɪts/ **36**
hiker /'haɪkər/ **92**
hiking /'haɪkɪŋ/ **92**
hill /hɪl/ **106**
hip /hɪp/ **31**
hip-bone /'hɪp bəʊn/ **32**
hippopotamus /ˌhɪpə'pɒtəməs/ **96**
history /'hɪstəri/ **53**
hoarding /'hɔːdɪŋ/ **75**
hob /hɒb/ **8**
hobbies /'hɒbiz/ **88**
hold /həʊld/ **35**
hole /həʊl/ **83**
hole-punch /'həʊl pʌntʃ/ **24**
home improvement /ˌhəʊm ɪm'pruːvmənt/ **88**
home page /'həʊm peɪdʒ/ **110**
honey /'hʌni/ **57**
honeycomb /'hʌnikəʊm/ **99**
hood /hʊd/ **46**
hooded top /ˌhʊdɪd 'tɒp/ **43**
hook /hʊk/ **26, 28**
hook and eye /ˌ. . './ **48**
hoover /'huːvər/ **19**
hop /hɒp/ **86**
horn /hɔːn/ **96**
hors d'oeuvres /ɔː 'dɜːv/ **60**
horse /hɔːs/ **83, 95**
horse racing /'hɔːs ˌreɪsɪŋ/ **81**
horse riding /'hɔːs ˌraɪdɪŋ/ **83**
hose /həʊz/ **17, 66, 79**
hosepipe /'həʊzpaɪp/ **17**
hospital porter /ˌhɒspɪtl 'pɔːtər/ **41**
hospital trolley /ˌhɒspɪtl 'trɒli/ **41**
hospital ward /'hɒspɪtl wɔːd/ **41**
hot /hɒt/ **107**
hot-air balloon /ˌhɒt 'eə bəˌluːn/ **92**
hot dog /ˌ. './ **61**
hotplate /'hɒtpleɪt/ **8**
hot water tap /. '.. ./ **10**
hot wax /hɒt 'wæks/ **36**
hour hand /'aʊə hænd/ **103**
household products /ˌhaʊshəʊld 'prɒdʌkts/ **58**
hug /hʌg/ **34**
Hull /hʌl/ **104**
hummingbird /'hʌmɪŋbɜːd/ **98**
hummus /'hʊmʊs/ **59**
hump /hʌmp/ **96**
husband /'hʌzbənd/ **5**
hutch /hʌtʃ/ **94**
hyacinth /'haɪəsɪnθ/ **16**
hyperlink /'haɪpəlɪŋk/ **110**
hypotenuse /haɪ'pɒtənjuːz/ **101**

ice /aɪs/ **85**
ice cream /'aɪs kriːm/ **57, 60, 61**
icon /'aɪkɒn/ **109**
icy /'aɪsi/ **107**
Idaho /'aɪdəhəʊ/ **105**

ignition /ɪg'nɪʃən/ **67**
Illinois /ˌɪlɪ'nɔɪ/ **105**
immigration officer /ˌɪmɪ'greɪʃən ˌɒfɪsər/ **70**
in /ɪn/ **115**
Indiana /ˌɪndi'ænə/ **105**
indicator /'ɪndɪkeɪtər/ **67**
information desk /ˌɪnfə'meɪʃən desk/ **54**
information section /ˌɪnfə'meɪʃən ˌsekʃən/ **54**
information technology /ˌɪnfə'meɪʃən tek,nɒlədʒi/ **53**
in front of /ɪn 'frʌnt ɒv/ **115**
in the middle of /ɪn ðə 'mɪdl ɒv/ **116**
in tray /'ɪn treɪ/ **24**
initials /ɪ'nɪʃəlz/ **4**
injection /ɪn'dʒekʃən/ **41**
injured person /ˌɪndʒəd 'pɜːsən/ **79**
in-line skate /ˌɪn laɪn 'skeɪt/ **83**
inmate /'ɪnmeɪt/ **30**
insect bite /'ɪnsekt baɪt/ **38, 39**
insect repellent /'ɪnsekt rɪˌpelənt/ **39**
insects /'ɪnsekts/ **99**
inside /ˌɪn'saɪd/ **116**
inside lane /ˌɪnsaɪd 'leɪn/ **68**
instrument panel /'ɪnstrəmənt ˌpænl/ **71**
intercom /'ɪntəkɒm/ **14**
international code /ˌɪntənæʃənəl 'kəʊd/ **79**
internet café /'ɪntənet ˌkæfeɪ/ **110**
internet service provider /ˌɪntənet 'sɜːvɪs prəˌvaɪdər/ **110**
interview /'ɪntəvjuː/ **20**
into /'ɪntuː/ **116**
Inverness /ˌɪnvə'nes/ **104**
Iowa /'aɪəwə/ **105**
iris /'aɪərɪs/ **16**
iron /'aɪən/ **15, 19**
ironing board /'aɪənɪŋ bɔːd/ **15**
iron-on tape /ˌaɪən ɒn 'teɪp/ **48**
irritated eyes /ˌɪrɪteɪtɪd 'aɪz/ **39**
island /'aɪlənd/ **106**
Isle of Man /ˌaɪl əv 'mæn/ **104**
Isle of Wight /ˌaɪl əv 'waɪt/ **104**
isosceles triangle /aɪˌsɒsəliːz 'traɪæŋgəl/ **101**
IT /ˌaɪ 'tiː/ **53**

jacket /'dʒækɪt/ **43, 44, 45**
jam /dʒæm/ **57, 64**
January /'dʒænjuəri/ **102**
jar /dʒɑːr/ **62**
jeans /dʒiːnz/ **44, 45**
jet engine /dʒet 'endʒɪn/ **71**
jet (plane) /'dʒet pleɪn/ **71**
jewellery /'dʒuːəlri/ **49**
jigsaw puzzle /'dʒɪgsɔː ˌpʌzəl/ **51**

job board /'dʒɒb bɔːd/ **20**
jockey /'dʒɒki/ **81**
jogger /'dʒɒgər/ **83**
jogging /'dʒɒgɪŋ/ **83**
journal /'dʒɜːnl/ **54**
journalist /'dʒɜːnəl-ɪst/ **23**
joystick /'dʒɔɪˌstɪk/ **109**
judge /dʒʌdʒ/ **22, 30**
judo /'dʒuːdəʊ/ **82**
jug /dʒʌg/ **13**
July /dʒʊ'laɪ/ **102**
jumper /'dʒʌmpər/ **45**
junction /'dʒʌŋkʃən/ **68**
June /dʒuːn/ **102**
junior school /'dʒuːniə skuːl/ **50**
Jupiter /'dʒuːpɪtər/ **108**
jury /'dʒʊəri/ **30**

kangaroo /ˌkæŋgə'ruː/ **96**
Kansas /'kænzəs/ **105**
karate /kə'rɑːti/ **82**
kennel /'kenl/ **94**
Kentucky /ken'tʌki/ **105**
kerb /kɜːb/ **74**
ketchup /'ketʃəp/ **58**
kettle /'ketl/ **9**
keyboard /'kiːbɔːd/ **109**
keyboards /'kiːbɔːdz/ **90**
keypad /'kiːpæd/ **112**
key ring /'kiː rɪŋ/ **49**
keyword /'kiːwɜːd/ **110**
kick /kɪk/ **86**
kid /kɪd/ **95**
kidney /'kɪdni/ **32**
kilogram /'kɪləgræm/ **62**
kiosk /'kiːɒsk/ **65**
kiss /kɪs/ **34**
kitchen /'kɪtʃɪn/ **8**
kitchen unit /'kɪtʃɪn ˌjuːnɪt/ **8**
kite /kaɪt/ **51**
kitten /'kɪtn/ **94**
kiwi fruit /'kiːwi fruːt/ **56**
knead /niːd/ **63**
knee /niː/ **31**
kneecap /'niːkæp/ **32**
kneel /niːl/ **86**
knickers /'nɪkəz/ **44**
knife /naɪf/ **9, 13**
knitting /'nɪtɪŋ/ **88**
knitting needle /'nɪtɪŋ ˌniːdl/ **48, 88**
knocker /'nɒkər/ **7**
koala bear /kəʊˌɑːlə 'beər/ **96**

ladder /'lædər/ **28, 79**
ladle /'leɪdl/ **9**
ladybird /'leɪdibɜːd/ **99**
lake /leɪk/ **106**
Lake Erie /leɪk 'ɪəri/ **105**
Lake Huron /leɪk 'hjʊərɒn/ **105**
Lake Michigan /leɪk 'mɪʃɪgən/ **105**
Lake Ontario /leɪk ɒn'teəriəʊ/ **105**
Lake Superior /leɪk suː'pɪəriər/ **105**
lamb /læm/ **95**
lamb chops /læm 'tʃɒps/ **59**
lamp /læmp/ **11, 12, 42**

lamp post /'læmp pəʊst/ **68**
lampshade /'læmpʃeɪd/ **12**
landing /'lændɪŋ/ **18, 71**
language lab booth
    /'læŋgwɪdʒ læb buːð/ **52**
lapel /lə'pel/ **46**
laptop /'læptɒp/ **109**
large intestine /lɑːdʒ ɪn'testɪn/
    32
lasagne /lə'sænjə/ **60**
Latin /'lætɪn/ **53**
laugh /lɑːf/ **34**
launch pad /'lɔːntʃ pæd/ **108**
laundry basket /'lɔːndri
    ˌbɑːskɪt/ **10, 15**
lawn /lɔːn/ **16**
lawn mower /'lɔːn ˌməʊə/ **17**
lawyer /'lɔːjə/ **22**
leather /'leðə/ **48**
lecture /'lektʃə/ **54**
lecture hall /'lektʃə hɔːl/ **54**
lecturer /'lektʃərə/ **22, 54**
lecturer's/tutor's office
    /'lektʃərəz ˌɒfɪs, 'tjuːtəz
    ˌɒfɪs/ **54**
Leeds /liːdz/ **104**
leek /liːk/ **55**
leg /leg/ **31**
leg of lamb /ˌ.. './ **59**
leggings /'legɪŋz/ **44**
lemon /'lemən/ **56**
lemonade /ˌlemə'neɪd/ **58**
lending desk /'lendɪŋ desk/ **54**
length /leŋθ/ **101**
lens /lenz/ **42, 112**
leopard /'lepəd/ **96**
leotard /'liːətɑːd/ **83**
letter /'letə/ **76**
letterbox /'letəbɒks/ **7, 76**
lettuce /'letɪs/ **55**
level crossing /ˌlevəl 'krɒsɪŋ/
    69
level crossing sign
    /ˌlevəl 'krɒsɪŋ saɪn/ **69**
librarian /laɪ'breəriən/ **54**
library /'laɪbrəri/ **54**
library assistant
    /'laɪbrəri əˌsɪstənt/ **54**
library card /'laɪbrəri ˌkɑːd/ **54**
lid /lɪd/ **9**
lie down /laɪ 'daʊn/ **34**
life jacket /'laɪf ˌdʒækɪt/ **71,
    72**
lifeboat /'laɪfbəʊt/ **72**
lifeguard /'laɪfgɑːd/ **91**
lift /lɪft/ **29, 86**
light /laɪt/ **114**
light blue /laɪt 'bluː/ **47**
light bulb /'laɪt bʌlb/ **112**
lighthouse /'laɪthaʊs/ **72**
lightning and thunder
    /ˌlaɪtnɪŋ ən 'θʌndə/ **107**
Li-lo™ /'laɪ ləʊ/ **91**
lily /'lɪli/ **16**
lime /laɪm/ **56**
Limerick /'lɪmərɪk/ **104**
line AmE /laɪn/ **93**
linen /'lɪnɪn/ **48**
liner /'laɪnə/ **72**
lines /laɪnz/ **101**
lion /'laɪən/ **96**

lip balm /'lɪp bɑːm/ **39**
lips /lɪps/ **31**
lipstick /'lɪpˌstɪk/ **37**
listen to the radio
    /ˌlɪsən tə ðə 'reɪdiəʊ/ **6**
litre /'liːtə/ **62**
litter bin /'lɪtə bɪn/ **75**
liver /'lɪvə/ **32, 59**
Liverpool /'lɪvəpuːl/ **104**
living room /'lɪvɪŋ ruːm/ **18**
lizard /'lɪzəd/ **96**
llama /'lɑːmə/ **96**
load the dishwasher
    /ˌləʊd ðə 'dɪʃwɒʃə/ **19**
loading dock/bay
    /'ləʊdɪŋ dɒk, 'ləʊdɪŋ beɪ/ **27**
loaf /ləʊf/ **62**
lobster /'lɒbstə/ **59, 97**
loft /lɒft/ **18**
lollipop /'lɒlipɒp/ **77**
London /'lʌndən/ **104**
Londonderry /'lʌndənderi/ **104**
long /lɒŋ/ **114**
long hair /ˌlɒŋ 'heə/ **33**
long-sleeved /ˌlɒŋ 'sliːvd/ **46**
loose /luːs/ **46, 114**
lorry /'lɒri/ **66, 68**
lorry driver /'lɒri ˌdraɪvə/ **21**
Los Angeles /lɒs 'ændʒəliːz/
    105
Louisiana /luˌiːzi'ænə/ **105**
lounge /laʊndʒ/ **18**
luggage /'lʌgɪdʒ/ **70**
luggage compartment
    /'lʌgɪdʒ kəmˌpɑːtmənt/ **65**
luggage trolley /'lʌgɪdʒ ˌtrɒli/
    70
lunar module /ˌluːnə 'mɒdjuːl/
    108
lunar vehicle /ˌluːnə 'viːɪkəl/
    108
lunch /lʌntʃ/ **64**
lung /lʌŋ/ **32**
lychee /'laɪtʃi/ **56**

machine /mə'ʃiːn/ **27**
magazine /ˌmægə'ziːn/ **77**
magnifying glass
    /'mægnɪfaɪ-ɪŋ glɑːs/ **88**
main courses /'meɪn ˌkɔːsɪz/
    60
Maine /meɪn/ **105**
make breakfast
    /meɪk 'brekfəst/ **19**
make lunch/dinner /meɪk
    'lʌntʃ, meɪk 'dɪnə/ **19**
make the bed /ˌmeɪk ðə 'bed/
    19
make-up /'meɪk ʌp/ **36**
make-up bag /'.. ./ **49**
mallet /'mælɪt/ **26**
man /mæn/ **4**
Manchester /'mæntʃɪstə/ **104**
mane /meɪn/ **96**
mango /'mæŋgəʊ/ **56**
manhole cover
    /'mænhəʊl ˌkʌvə/ **75**
manicure items
    /'mænɪkjʊə ˌaɪtəmz/ **37**
mantelpiece /'mæntlpiːs/ **12**
March /mɑːtʃ/ **102**

margarine /ˌmɑːdʒə'riːn/ **57**
marina /mə'riːnə/ **72**
marital status /ˌmærɪtl 'steɪtəs/
    4
marmalade /'mɑːməleɪd/ **64**
married /'mærid/ **4**
Mars /mɑːz/ **108**
Maryland /'meərɪlənd/ **105**
mascara /mæ'skɑːrə/ **37**
mask /mɑːsk/ **41, 84**
Massachusetts
    /ˌmæsə'tʃuːsəts/ **105**
mast /mɑːst/ **72, 84**
master bedroom
    /ˌmɑːstə 'bedruːm/ **18**
Master of Arts (MA)
    /ˌmɑːstər əv 'ɑːts, ˌem 'eɪ/
    50
Master of Science (MSc)
    /ˌmɑːstər əv 'saɪəns, ˌem es
    'siː/ **50**
mat /mæt/ **52, 82, 86**
matches /'mætʃɪz/ **77**
maths /mæθs/ **53**
mattress /'mætrəs/ **11**
May /meɪ/ **102**
May Day (May 1st)
    /'meɪ deɪ, ˌmeɪ ðə 'fɜːst/
    102
mayonnaise /ˌmeɪə'neɪz/ **58**
meadow /'medəʊ/ **106**
measure ingredients
    /ˌmeʒər ɪn'griːdiənts/ **63**
measuring beaker
    /'meʒərɪŋ ˌbiːkə/ **52**
measuring cylinder
    /'meʒərɪŋ ˌsɪlɪndə/ **52**
measuring jug
    /'meʒərɪŋ dʒʌg/ **9**
measuring spoon
    /'meʒərɪŋ spuːn/ **9**
meat /miːt/ **59**
mechanic /mɪ'kænɪk/ **21**
medical chart /'medɪkəl tʃɑːt/
    41
medical records
    /ˌmedɪkəl 'rekɔːdz/ **40**
medical specialists
    /ˌmedɪkəl 'speʃəlɪsts/ **40**
melon /'melən/ **56, 60**
menu /'menjuː/ **60**
Mercury /'mɜːkjʊri/ **108**
messy /'mesi/ **114**
metal detector
    /'metl dɪˌtektə/ **70**
metals /'metlz/ **49**
metre /'miːtə/ **62**
Miami /maɪ'æmi/ **105**
Michigan /'mɪʃɪgən/ **105**
microfiche /'maɪkrəʊfiːʃ/ **54**
microfiche reader
    /'maɪkrəʊfiːʃ ˌriːdə/ **54**
microphone /'maɪkrəfəʊn/ **90**
microwave
    /'maɪkrəweɪv/ **9**
middle lane /ˌmɪdl 'leɪn/ **68**
middle school /'mɪdl skuːl/ **50**
mike /maɪk/ **90**
milk /mɪlk/ **57, 60**
milk shake /mɪlk 'ʃeɪk/ **61**
millilitres /'mɪliˌliːtəz/ **62**

millimetre /'mɪliˌmiːtə/ **62**
minced beef /ˌmɪnst 'biːf/ **59**
mineral water
    /'mɪnərəl ˌwɔːtə/ **58**
minibus /'mɪnibʌs/ **66**
minicab /'mɪnikæb/ **65**
Minnesota /ˌmɪnə'səʊtə/ **105**
mints /mɪnts/ **77**
minute hand /'mɪnɪt hænd/ **103**
mirror /'mɪrə/ **10, 11, 36, 42**
miserable /'mɪzərəbəl/ **113**
missing button /ˌmɪsɪŋ 'bʌtn/
    48
Mississippi /ˌmɪsɪ'sɪpi/ **105**
Mississippi River /ˌ.... '../ **105**
Missouri /mɪ'zʊəri/ **105**
Missouri River /ˌ.ˌ. '../ **105**
mix /mɪks/ **63**
mixed vegetables
    /ˌmɪkst 'vedʒtəbəlz/ **60**
mixing bowl /'mɪksɪŋ bəʊl/ **9**
mobile /'məʊbaɪl/ **14, 112**
modem /'məʊdem/ **109**
moisturiser /'mɔɪstʃəraɪzə/ **37**
mole /məʊl/ **99**
Monday /'mʌndi/ **102**
money clip /'mʌni klɪp/ **49**
monitor /'mɒnɪtə/ **109**
monkey /'mʌŋki/ **96**
Monopoly™ /mə'nɒpəli/ **89**
Montana /mɒn'tænə/ **105**
month /mʌnθ/ **102**
moon /muːn/ **108**
mop /mɒp/ **15**
mosquito /mɒ'skiːtəʊ/ **99**
moth /mɒθ/ **99**
mother /'mʌðə/ **5**
mother-in-law /'mʌðər ɪn lɔː/
    5
Mother's Day /'mʌðəz deɪ/
    102
motor boat /'məʊtə bəʊt/ **72**
motorbike /'məʊtəbaɪk/ **66**
motorboat /'məʊtəbəʊt/ **84**
motorcycle courier
    /'məʊtəˌsaɪkəl ˌkʊriə/ **21**
motor scooter
    /'məʊtə ˌskuːtə/ **66**
motorway /'məʊtəweɪ/ **68**
mountain /'maʊntɪn/ **106**
mouse /maʊs/ **99, 109**
mouse mat /'maʊs mæt/ **109**
moustache /mə'stɑːʃ‖'mʌstæʃ/
    33
mouth /maʊθ/ **31**
mouthwash /'maʊθwɒʃ/ **42**
movie AmE /'muːvi/ **87**
mow the lawn /ˌməʊ ðə 'lɔːn/
    17
muesli /'mjuːzli/ **64**
muffin /'mʌfɪn/ **61**
mug /mʌg/ **10**
muscles /'mʌsəlz/ **32**
museum /mjuː'ziːəm/ **93**
mushroom /'mʌʃruːm/ **55**
music /'mjuːzɪk/ **53**
music shop /'mjuːzɪk ʃɒp/ **78**
music stand /'mjuːzɪk
    stænd/ **87**
mussels /'mʌsəlz/ **59, 97**
mustard /'mʌstəd/ **58, 61**

WORDLIST

naan bread /'nɑːn bred/ **59**
nail /neɪl/ **26, 31**
nail clippers /'neɪl ˌklɪpəz/ **37**
nail file /'neɪl faɪl/ **37**
nail polish /'neɪl ˌpɒlɪʃ/ **37**
nail scissors /'neɪl ˌsɪzəz/ **37**
nail varnish /'neɪl ˌvɑːnɪʃ/ **37**
name /neɪm/ **4**
nanny goat /'næni gəʊt/ **95**
napkin /'næpkɪn/ **13**
napkin ring /'næpkɪn rɪŋ/ **13**
nappy /'næpi/ **14**
narrow /'nærəʊ/ **46, 114**
nature reserve /'neɪtʃə rɪˌzɜːv/ **92**
navy blue /ˌneɪvi 'bluː/ **47**
near /nɪər/ **114**
neat /niːt/ **114**
Nebraska /nɪ'bræskə/ **105**
neck /nek/ **31**
neck and shoulder massage /ˌnek ən 'ʃəʊldə ˌmæsɑːʒ/ **36**
necklaces /'neklɪsɪz/ **49**
nectarine /'nektəriːn/ **56**
needle /'niːdl/ **41, 48**
nephew /'nefjuː/ **5**
Neptune /'neptjuːn/ **108**
nervous /'nɜːvəs/ **113**
nest /nest/ **98**
net /net/ **80, 81, 82**
network /'netwɜːk/ **110**
Nevada /nə'vɑːdə/ **105**
Newcastle-upon-Tyne /ˌnjuːkɑːsəl əpɒn 'taɪn/ **104**
New Hampshire /njuː 'hæmpʃər/ **105**
New Jersey /njuː 'dʒɜːzi/ **105**
New Mexico /njuː 'meksɪkəʊ/ **105**
new moon /njuː 'muːn/ **108**
New Orleans /njuː 'ɔːliənz/ **105**
newspaper /'njuːsˌpeɪpər/ **29, 77**
newspaper stand /'njuːspeɪpə ˌstænd/ **75**
newspaper vendor /'njuːspeɪpə ˌvendər/ **75**
newsreader /'njuːzˌriːdər/ **23**
New Year's Eve /ˌnjuː jɪəz 'iːv/ **102**
New York /njuː 'jɔːk/ **105**
next of kin /ˌnekst əv 'kɪn/ **4**
next to /'nekst tuː/ **116**
niece /niːs/ **5**
nightclothes /'naɪtkləʊðz/ **43**
nightdress /'naɪtdres/ **43**
nightie /'naɪti/ **43**
nine /naɪn/ **100**
nineteen /ˌnaɪn'tiːn/ **100**
nineteen thirty /ˌnaɪntiːn 'θɜːti/ **103**
ninety /'naɪnti/ **100**
nineteen forty-five /ˌ.. .. './ **103**
no overtaking sign /nəʊ əʊvə'teɪkɪŋ saɪn/ **69**
no right turn sign /nəʊ raɪt 'tɜːn saɪn/ **69**

North Carolina /ˌnɔːθ kærə'laɪnə/ **105**
North Dakota /ˌnɔːθ də'kəʊtə/ **105**
Northern Ireland /ˌnɔːðən 'aɪələnd/ **104**
nose /nəʊz/ **31**
nose bleed /'nəʊz bliːd/ **38**
note appointments /ˌnəʊt ə'pɔɪntmənts/ **25**
notepad /'nəʊtpæd/ **24**
no through road sign /nəʊ θruː 'rəʊd saɪn/ **69**
noticeboard /'nəʊtɪsˌbɔːd/ **24**
Nottingham /'nɒtɪŋəm/ **104**
no U-turn sign /nəʊ 'juː tɜːn saɪn/ **69**
November /nəʊ'vembər/ **102**
nozzle /'nɒzəl/ **66**
number pad /'nʌmbə pæd/ **79**
numberplate /'nʌmbəpleɪt/ **67**
nurse /nɜːs/ **22, 40, 41**
nursery assistant /'nɜːsəri əˌsɪstənt/ **22**
nursery school /'nɜːsəri skuːl/ **50**
nut /nʌt/ **26**
nuts and raisins /ˌnʌts ənd 'reɪzənz/ **61**

oak tree /'əʊk triː/ **106**
oar /ɔːr/ **72, 84**
oats /əʊts/ **58**
oboe /'əʊbəʊ/ **90**
obstetrician /ˌɒbstə'trɪʃən/ **40**
obtuse angle /əb'tjuːs ˌæŋgəl/ **101**
ocean AmE /'əʊʃən/ **91**
October /ɒk'təʊbər/ **102**
octopus /'ɒktəpəs/ **97**
off /ɒf/ **115**
offer refreshments /ˌɒfə rɪ'freʃmənts/ **25**
office worker /'ɒfɪs ˌwɜːkər/ **23**
offices /'ɒfɪsɪz/ **74**
Ohio /əʊ'haɪəʊ/ **105**
oil /ɔɪl/ **58**
oil tanker /'ɔɪl ˌtæŋkər/ **72**
Oklahoma /ˌəʊklə'həʊmə/ **105**
old /əʊld/ **4**
omelette /'ɒmlət/ **64**
on /ɒn/ **115**
on board /ɒn 'bɔːd/ **71**
one /wʌn/ **100**
one half/a half /wʌn 'hɑːf, ə 'hɑːf/ **62**
one hundred /wʌn 'hʌndrəd/ **100**
one hundred and one /. ˌ.. . './ **100**
one hundred percent /wʌn ˌhʌndrəd pə'sent/ **100**
one hundred thousand /wʌn ˌhʌndrəd 'θaʊzənd/ **100**
one million /wʌn 'mɪljən/ **100**
one penny/one penny piece /wʌn 'peni, ˌwʌn peni 'piːs/ **73**

one pound/one pound coin /wʌn 'paʊnd, ˌwʌn paʊnd 'kɔɪn/ **73**
one quarter /wʌn 'kwɔːtər/ **62**
one third /wʌn 'θɜːd/ **62**
one thousand /wʌn 'θaʊzənd/ **100**
onion /'ʌnjən/ **55**
online banking /ˌɒnlaɪn 'bæŋkɪŋ/ **73**
onto /'ɒntuː/ **115**
on top of /. '. ./ **116**
open /'əʊpən/ **35, 114**
opera /'ɒpərə/ **87**
operating theatre /'ɒpəreɪtɪŋ ˌθɪətər/ **41**
operation /ˌɒpə'reɪʃən/ **41**
ophthalmologist /ˌɒfθæl'mɒlədʒɪst/ **40**
opposites /'ɒpəzɪts/ **114**
optician /ɒp'tɪʃən/ **22, 42, 78**
oral hygienist /ˌɔːrəl 'haɪdʒiːnɪst/ **42**
orange /'ɒrɪndʒ/ **47, 56**
orange juice /'ɒrɪndʒ dʒuːs/ **58**
orbit /'ɔːbɪt/ **108**
orchestra pit /'ɔːkɪstrə pɪt/ **87**
orchid /'ɔːkɪd/ **16**
Oregon /'ɒrɪgən/ **105**
Orkney Islands /'ɔːkni ˌaɪləndz/ **104**
orthodontist /ˌɔːθə'dɒntɪst/ **42**
osteopath /'ɒstiəpæθ/ **40**
ostrich /'ɒstrɪtʃ/ **98**
other instruments /ˌʌðər 'ɪnstrəmənts/ **90**
other vehicles /ˌʌðə 'viːɪkəlz/ **66**
out /aʊt/ **115**
outdoor clothing /ˌaʊtdɔː 'kləʊðɪŋ/ **43**
out of /'aʊt əv/ **116**
outside /aʊt'saɪd, 'aʊtsaɪd/ **116**
outside lane /ˌaʊtsaɪd 'leɪn/ **68**
out tray /'aʊt treɪ/ **24**
oval /'əʊvəl/ **101**
oven /'ʌvən/ **8**
oven glove /'ʌvən glʌv/ **9**
over /'əʊvər/ **115**
overcast /ˌəʊvə'kɑːst/ **107**
overhead (luggage) compartment /ˌəʊvəhed 'lʌgɪdʒ kəmˌpɑːtmənt/ **71**
overhead projector /ˌəʊvəhed prə'dʒektər/ **52**
overweight /ˌəʊvə'weɪt/ **33**
owl /aʊl/ **98**
Oxford /'ɒksfəd/ **104**
oxygen mask /'ɒksɪdʒən ˌmɑːsk/ **71, 79**

Pacific Ocean /pəˌsɪfɪk 'əʊʃən/ **105**
package AmE /'pækɪdʒ/ **76**
packet /'pækɪt/ **62**
packet of crisps /ˌpækɪt əv 'krɪsps/ **77**
packet of envelopes /ˌpækɪt əv 'envələʊps/ **77**

paddle /'pædl/ **84**
pads /pædz/ **80, 83**
paediatrician /ˌpiːdiə'trɪʃən/ **40**
pager /'peɪdʒər/ **112**
pail AmE /peɪl/ **91**
painkillers /'peɪnˌkɪləz/ **39**
paint /peɪnt/ **26, 35**
paintbox /'peɪntbɒks/ **51**
paintbrush /'peɪntbrʌʃ/ **26, 51**
painter /'peɪntər/ **21**
painting /'peɪntɪŋ/ **88**
paint pot /'peɪnt pɒt/ **26**
paint roller /'peɪnt ˌrəʊlər/ **26**
paint tray /'peɪnt treɪ/ **26**
pallet /'pælət/ **27**
palm /pɑːm/ **31**
palm tree /'. ./ **106**
pansy /'pænzi/ **16**
panties AmE /'pæntiz/ **44**
pants AmE /pænts/ **44, 45**
papaya /pə'paɪə/ **56**
paperback /'peɪpəbæk/ **77**
paper clip holder /'peɪpə klɪp ˌhəʊldər/ **24**
paper clips /'peɪpə klɪps/ **24**
paper napkin /ˌpeɪpə 'næpkɪn/ **61**
parachute /'pærəʃuːt/ **83**
parachuting /'pærəˌʃuːtɪŋ/ **83**
parachutist /'pærəˌʃuːtɪst/ **83**
parallel /'pærəlel/ **101**
paramedic /ˌpærə'medɪk/ **79**
parasol /'pærəsɒl/ **16**
parcel /'pɑːsəl/ **76**
parent /'peərənt/ **5**
park /pɑːk/ **93**
parking meter /'pɑːkɪŋ ˌmiːtər/ **74**
parking notice /'pɑːkɪŋ ˌnəʊtɪs/ **74**
parrot /'pærət/ **98**
parsnip /'pɑːsnɪp/ **55**
parting /'pɑːtɪŋ/ **33**
passenger /'pæsɪndʒər/ **65**
passport /'pɑːspɔːt/ **70**
passport control /'pɑːspɔːt kənˌtrəʊl/ **70**
password /'pɑːswɜːd/ **110**
pasta /'pæstə/ **58**
path /pɑːθ/ **92**
patient /'peɪʃənt/ **40, 41, 42**
patio /'pætiəʊ/ **16**
patio chair /'pætiəʊ ˌtʃeər/ **16**
patio table /'pætiəʊ ˌteɪbəl/ **16**
pattern /'pætən/ **48**
patterned /'pætənd/ **47**
patterns /'pætənz/ **47**
pavement /'peɪvmənt/ **74**
paw /pɔː/ **94**
paying-in slip /ˌpeɪ-ɪŋ 'ɪn slɪp/ **73**
PC /ˌpiː 'siː/ **109**
PE /ˌpiː 'iː/ **53**
peach /piːtʃ/ **56**
peacock /'piːkɒk/ **98**
peak /piːk/ **106**
peanut /'piːnʌt/ **56**
peanuts /'piːnʌts/ **61**
pear /peər/ **56**
pearls /pɜːlz/ **49**

peas /piːz/ **55, 57**
pedestrian /pəˈdestriən/ **68, 74**
pedestrian underpass
/pəˌdestriən ˈʌndəpɑːs/ **68**
peel /piːl/ **63**
peeler /ˈpiːlər/ **9**
peg /peg/ **15**
pelican /ˈpelikən/ **98**
pelvis /ˈpelvis/ **32**
penalty box /ˈpenlti bɒks/ **80**
penalty spot /ˈpenlti spɒt/ **80**
pencil /ˈpensəl/ **24, 52, 77**
pencil sharpener
/ˈpensəl ˌʃɑːpənər/ **52**
penguin /ˈpeŋgwin/ **98**
Pennsylvania /ˌpensəlˈveiniə/
105
people carrier /ˈpiːpəl ˌkæriər/
66
pepper /ˈpepər/ **13, 58**
percussion /pəˈkʌʃən/ **90**
performing arts
/pəˌfɔːmiŋ ˈɑːts/ **53**
perfume /ˈpɜːfjuːm/ **37**
periodicals and books
/ˌpiəriˌɒdikəlz ənd ˈbuks/ **77**
periodical section
/ˌpiəriˈɒdikəl ˌsekʃən/ **54**
perm /pɜːm/ **36**
perpendicular
/ˌpɜːpənˈdikjulər/ **101**
personal assistant (PA)
/ˌpɜːsənəl əˈsistənt, ˌpiː ˈei/
23
personal banker
/ˌpɜːsənəl ˈbæŋkər/ **73**
personal cassette player
/ˌpɜːsənəl kəˈset ˌpleiər/
111
personal computer
/ˌpɜːsənəl kəmˈpjuːtər/ **109**
personal organizer
/ˌpɜːsənəl ˈɔːgənaizər/ **49**
petrol cap /ˈpetrəl kæp/ **67**
petrol pump /ˈpetrəl pʌmp/ **66**
petrol station /ˈpetrəl ˌsteiʃən/
66
petunia /pəˈtjuːniə/ **16**
pharmacist /ˈfɑːməsist/ **22**
pheasant /ˈfezənt/ **98**
phone box /ˈfəun bɒks/ **75**
phonecard /ˈfəunkɑːd/ **79**
photocopier /ˈfəutəuˌkɒpiər/
24, 54
photocopy a letter
/ˌfəutəukɒpi ə ˈletər/ **25**
photographer /fəˈtɒgrəfər/ **23**
photography /fəˈtɒgrəfi/ **88**
physical education
/ˌfizikəl edjuˈkeiʃən/ **53**
physics /ˈfiziks/ **53**
physiotherapist
/ˌfiziəuˈθerəpist/ **40**
piano /piˈænəu/ **90**
piccolo /ˈpikələu/ **90**
pickaxe /ˈpik-æks/ **28**
pick up /ˌpik ˈʌp/ **35**
pick up the children
/ˌpik ʌp ðə ˈtʃildrən/ **19**
picnic /ˈpiknik/ **92**
picture /ˈpiktʃər/ **12**

picture frame /ˈpiktʃə freim/ **12**
pieces /ˈpiːsiz/ **89**
pie /pai/ **59**
pier /piər/ **91**
pig /pig/ **95**
pigeon /ˈpidʒin/ **98**
piglet /ˈpiglət/ **95**
pillar box /ˈpilə bɒks/ **76**
pillow /ˈpiləu/ **11**
pillowcase /ˈpiləukeis/ **11**
pilot /ˈpailət/ **71**
pin /pin/ **48**
pin cushion /ˈpin ˌkuʃən/ **48**
pineapple /ˈpainæpəl/ **56**
pin number /ˈpin ˌnʌmbər/ **73**
ping-pong /ˈpiŋ pɒŋ/ **82**
ping-pong ball /ˈ. . ˌ./ **82**
ping-pong player /ˈ. . ˌ../ **82**
ping-pong table /ˈ. . ˌ../ **82**
pink /piŋk/ **47**
pipette /piˈpet/ **52**
pitch /pitʃ/ **80**
pitta bread /ˈpitə bred/ **59**
pizza /ˈpiːtsə/ **57, 60**
place mat /ˈpleis mæt/ **13**
place of birth /ˌpleis əv ˈbɜːθ/
4
plain /plein/ **47**
plait /plæt/ **33**
plane /plein/ **26**
plant /plɑːnt/ **12**
plant flowers /plɑːnt ˈflauəz/
17
plant pot /ˈplɑːnt pɒt/ **12**
plaque /plɑːk, plæk/ **42**
plaster cast /ˈplɑːstə kɑːst/ **41**
plasters /ˈplɑːstəz/ **39**
plate /pleit/ **13**
platform /ˈplætfɔːm/ **65**
platform entrance
/ˌplætfɔːm ˈentrəns/ **65**
player /ˈpleiər/ **80**
pleased /pliːzd/ **113**
pliers /ˈplaiəz/ **26**
ploughman's lunch
/ˌplaumənz ˈlʌntʃ/ **61**
plug /plʌg/ **15**
plum /plʌm/ **56**
plumber /ˈplʌmər/ **21**
Pluto /ˈpluːtəu/ **108**
Plymouth /ˈpliməθ/ **104**
pneumatic drill
/njuːˌmætik ˈdril/ **28**
pocket /ˈpɒkit/ **46**
pocket calculator /ˌ.. ˈ..../ **112**
podium /ˈpəudiəm/ **87**
point /pɔint/ **34**
polar bear /ˌpəulə ˈbeər/ **96**
Polaroid™ camera
/ˌpəulərɔid ˈkæmərə/ **112**
pole /pəul/ **85**
police /pəˈliːs/ **79**
police car /.ˈ. ./ **79**
police officer /pəˈliːs ˌɒfisər/
22, 30, 79
police station /pəˈliːs ˌsteiʃən/
79
poloneck /ˈpəuləunek/ **43**
polyester /ˈpɒliestər/ **48**
pommel horse /ˈpʌməl hɔːs/
52

pond /pɒnd/ **16, 106**
pony /ˈpəuni/ **94**
pony tail /ˈ.. ./ **33**
pony trekking /ˈpəuni ˌtrekiŋ/
92
pop music /ˈpɒp ˌmjuːzik/ **90**
popper /ˈpɒpər/ **48**
porch /pɔːtʃ/ **7**
pork chops /ˌpɔːk ˈtʃɒps/ **59**
porridge /ˈpɒridʒ/ **64**
porter /ˈpɔːtər/ **29, 70**
postal order /ˈpəustl ˌɔːdər/ **76**
postbag /ˈpəustbæg/ **76**
postbox /ˈpəust bɒks/ **76**
postcard /ˈpəustkɑːd/ **76**
postcode /ˈpəustkəud/ **4, 76**
Post-it notes /ˈpəust it ˌnəuts/
24
postman /ˈpəustmən/ **22, 76**
postmark /ˈpəustmɑːk/ **76**
post office clerk
/ˈpəust ɒfis ˌklɑːkǁ-ˌklɜːrk/
76
Post Office van
/ˈpəust ɒfis ˌvæn/ **76**
posts /pəusts/ **80**
postwoman /ˈpəustˌwumən/
22, 76
pot /pɒt/ **17**
potato /pəˈteitəu/ **55**
potter's wheel /ˌpɒtəz ˈwiːl/
88
pottery /ˈpɒtəri/ **88**
potting shed /ˈpɒtiŋ ʃed/ **17**
potty /ˈpɒti/ **14**
pouch /pautʃ/ **96**
pour /pɔːr/ **35, 63**
power drill /ˈpauə dril/ **26**
power saw /ˈpauə sɔː/ **26**
pram /præm/ **14**
prawn cocktail /ˌprɔːn ˈkɒkteil/
60
prawns /prɔːnz/ **59**
pre-school /ˌpriː ˈskuːl/ **50, 51**
prescription /priˈskripʃən/ **40**
press /pres/ **35**
press stud /ˈpres stʌd/ **48**
primary school /ˈpraiməri
skuːl/ **50, 53**
print a hard copy
/ˌprint ə ˌhɑːd ˈkɒpi/ **25**
printer /ˈprintər/ **109**
prison /ˈprizən/ **30**
prison officer /ˈprizən ˌɒfisər/
30
private school /ˈpraivit skuːl/
50
promenade /ˌprɒməˈnɑːd/
91
protractor /prəˈtræktər/ **52**
prune /pruːn/ **56**
prune a shrub /ˌpruːn ə ˈʃrʌb/
17
public school /ˌpʌblik ˈskuːl/
50
pull /pul/ **34**
pump AmE /pʌmp/ **43**
pupil /ˈpjuːpəl/ **32, 52**
puppy /ˈpʌpi/ **94**
purple /ˈpɜːpəl/ **47**
purse /pɜːs/ **49**

push /puʃ/ **34**
pushchair /ˈpuʃ-tʃeər/ **14**
put down /put ˈdaun/ **35**
put on make-up
/ˌput ɒn ˈmeik ʌp/ **6**
pyjamas /pəˈdʒɑːməz/ **43**

queue /kjuː/ **93**
quilt /kwilt/ **11**

rabbit /ˈræbit/ **94, 95**
racehorse /ˈreishɔːs/ **81**
radiator /ˈreidieitər/ **11**
radio /ˈreidiəu/ **67, 111**
radish /ˈrædiʃ/ **55**
radius /ˈreidiəs/ **101**
railings /ˈreiliŋz/ **74**
railway station
/ˈreilwei ˌsteiʃən/ **65**
railway track /ˈreilwei ˌtræk/
69
rainbow /ˈreinbəu/ **107**
raincoat /ˈreinkəut/ **43**
rain hat /ˈrein hæt/ **43**
rainy /ˈreini/ **107**
raisin /ˈreizən/ **56**
rake /reik/ **17**
ram /ræm/ **95**
rambling /ˈræmbliŋ/ **92**
rash /ræʃ/ **38**
raspberry /ˈrɑːzbəri/ **56**
rat /ræt/ **99**
razor /ˈreizər/ **10, 37**
razor blade /ˈreizə bleid/ **37**
RE /ˌɑːr ˈiː/ **53**
reach /riːtʃ/ **86**
read /riːd/ **35**
read (the paper)
/ˌriːd ðə ˈpeipər/ **6**
rear windscreen
/riə ˈwindskriːn/ **67**
rearview mirror /ˌriəvjuː
ˈmirər/ **67**
receiver /riˈsiːvər/ **79**
reception /riˈsepʃən/ **29, 50**
receptionist /riˈsepʃənist/ **23,
29**
Recorded Delivery
/riˌkɔːdid diˈlivəri/ **76**
recorder /riˈkɔːdər/ **90**
rectangle /ˈrektæŋgəl/ **101**
red /red/ **47, 68**
red card /ˌred ˈkɑːd/ **80**
red hair /ˌred ˈheər/ **33**
red pepper /red ˈpepər/ **55**
red squirrel /red ˈskwirəl/ **99**
red wine /red ˈwain/ **58, 60**
referee /ˌrefəˈriː/ **80, 81**
reference section
/ˈrefərəns ˌsekʃən/ **54**
refrigerator /riˈfridʒəreitər/ **8**
refuse collector
/ˈrefjuːs kəˌlektər/ **21**
reins /reinz/ **83**
religious studies
/riˈlidʒəs ˌstʌdiz/ **53**
remarried /riːˈmærid/ **5**
remote control
/riˌməut kənˈtrəul/ **12, 111**
Republic of Ireland
/riˌpʌblik əv ˈaiələnd/ **104**

reservoir /'rezəvwɑːr/ 106
restaurant /'restərɒnt/ 29
résumé AmE /'rezjumeɪ/ 20
return ticket /rɪˌtɜːn 'tɪkɪt/ 65
rev counter /'rev ˌkaʊntər/ 67
rhinoceros /raɪ'nɒsərəs/ 96
Rhode Island /'rəʊd aɪlənd/ 105
rhubarb /'ruːbɑːb/ 56
ribs /rɪbz/ 32
rice /raɪs/ 58
ride /raɪd/ 93
rider /'raɪdər/ 83
right angle /'raɪt æŋgəl/ 101
right-angled triangle /ˌraɪt æŋgəld 'traɪæŋgəl/ 101
ring /rɪŋ/ 49, 81
rinse /rɪns/ 36
rinse your face /ˌ.. '.'./ 6
rip /rɪp/ 48
river /'rɪvər/ 75, 106
road accident /'rəʊd ˌæksɪdənt/ 79
roadsign /'rəʊdsaɪn/ 69, 74
roadworks /'rəʊdwɜːks/ 69
roadworks ahead sign /ˌrəʊdwɜːks ə'hed saɪn/ 69
roast /rəʊst/ 63
roast beef with Yorkshire pudding /rəʊst ˌbiːf wɪð ˌjɔːkʃə 'pʊdɪŋ/ 60
roast potatoes /ˌrəʊst pə'teɪtəʊz/ 60
roasting tin /'rəʊstɪŋ ˌtɪn/ 9
robin /'rɒbɪn/ 98
rock /rɒk/ 106
rock concert /'rɒkˌkɒnsət/ 87
Rocky Mountains /ˌrɒki 'maʊntɪnz/ 105
roll /rəʊl/ 62
roller /'rəʊlər/ 36
rollerblade /'rəʊləbleɪd/ 83
rollerblader /'rəʊləˌbleɪdər/ 83
rollerblading /'rəʊləˌbleɪdɪŋ/ 83
roller coaster /'rəʊlə ˌkəʊstər/ 93
roller skates /'rəʊlə skeɪts/ 51
rolling pin /'rəʊlɪŋ pɪn/ 9
roof /ruːf/ 7
roof-rack /'ruːf ræk/ 67
room key /'ruːm kiː/ 29
room service /'ruːm ˌsɜːvɪs/ 29
rope /rəʊp/ 81
rose /rəʊz/ 16
rotary whisk /'rəʊtəri wɪsk/ 9
rotor /'rəʊtər/ 71
rouge /ruːʒ/ 37
rough /rʌf/ 114
round /raʊnd/ 116
roundabout /'raʊndəbaʊt/ 68
roundabout sign /'raʊndəbaʊt saɪn/ 69
rounded scissors /ˌraʊndɪd 'sɪzəz/ 51
rower /'rəʊər/ 84
rowing /'rəʊɪŋ/ 84
rowing boat /'rəʊɪŋ bəʊt/ 72, 84

rowing machine /'.. .ˌ./ 86
rub /rʌb/ 63
rub in /.'.'./ 63
rubber /'rʌbər/ 24, 52, 77
rubber band /ˌrʌbə 'bænd/ 24
ruby /'ruːbi/ 49
rucksack /'rʌksæk/ 92
rug /rʌg/ 12
rugby /'rʌgbi/ 80
ruler /'ruːlər/ 52
run /rʌn/ 86
runner /'rʌnər/ 83
runner bean /ˌrʌnə 'biːn/ 55
running /'rʌnɪŋ/ 83
running machine /'.. .ˌ./ 86
runway /'rʌnweɪ/ 71
rush hour /'rʌʃ aʊər/ 65

sachet of pepper /ˌsæʃeɪ əv 'pepər/ 61
sachet of salt /ˌsæʃeɪ əv 'sɔːlt/ 61
sad /sæd/ 113
saddle /'sædl/ 83
safari park /sə'fɑːri pɑːk/ 93
safety glasses /'seɪfti ˌglɑːsɪz/ 27
safety pin /'seɪfti pɪn/ 48
sail /seɪl/ 84
sailboard /'seɪlbɔːd/ 84
sailboat AmE /'seɪlbəʊt/ 72
sailing /'seɪlɪŋ/ 84
sailing boat /'seɪlɪŋ bəʊt/ 84
sailing ship /'seɪlɪŋ ʃɪp/ 72
salad dressing /'sæləd ˌdresɪŋ/ 58
sales assistant /'seɪlz ˌəsɪstənt/ 23
salmon steaks /ˌsæmən 'steɪks/ 59
saloon car /sə'luːn kɑːr/ 66
salt /sɔːlt/ 13, 58
San Francisco /ˌsæn frən'sɪskəʊ/ 105
sand /sænd/ 51, 91
sandals /'sændlz/ 43
sandcastle /'sænd,kɑːsəl/ 91
sand dune /'sænd djuːn/ 106
sandpaper /'sænd,peɪpər/ 26
sandpit /'sænd,pɪt/ 51
sandwiches /'sænwɪdʒɪz/ 64
sapphire /'sæfaɪər/ 49
satellite /'sætəlaɪt/ 108
satellite dish /'sætəlaɪt dɪʃ/ 7
satellite TV /ˌsætəlaɪt tiː 'viː/ 111
satsuma /sæt'suːmə/ 56
Saturday /'sætədi/ 102
Saturn /'sætən/ 108
saucepan /'sɔːspæn/ 9
saucer /'sɔːsər/ 13
sausage /'sɒsɪdʒ/ 59
sauté /'səʊteɪ/ 63
saxophone /'sæksəfəʊn/ 90
scaffolding /'skæfəldɪŋ/ 28
scales /skeɪlz/ 40, 76, 97
scalpel /'skælpəl/ 41
scanner /'skænər/ 41, 109
scar /skɑːr/ 38
scared /skeəd/ 113

scarf /skɑːf/ 49
scatter cushion /'skætə ˌkʊʃən/ 11
science /'saɪəns/ 53
scientist /'saɪəntɪst/ 22
scissors /'sɪzəz/ 36, 48, 76
scooter /'skuːtər/ 51
scoreboard /'skɔːbɔːd/ 80
Scotland /'skɒtlənd/ 104
Scrabble™ /'skræbəl/ 89
scratch /skrætʃ/ 38
screen /skriːn/ 111
screw /skruː/ 26
screwdriver /'skruːˌdraɪvər/ 26
scrubbing brush /'skrʌbɪŋ brʌʃ/ 15
scuba diver /'skuːbə ˌdaɪvər/ 84
scuba diving /'skuːbəˌdaɪvɪŋ/ 84
sculpting /'skʌlptɪŋ/ 88
sculpture /'skʌlptʃər/ 88
sea /siː/ 91
sea animals /'siː ˌænɪməlz/ 97
seafood /'siːfuːd/ 59
seal /siːl/ 97
seam /siːm/ 46
search engine /'sɜːtʃ ˌendʒɪn/ 110
search page /'sɜːtʃ peɪdʒ/ 110
seasons /'siːzənz/ 107
seatbelt /'siːtbelt/ 67
Seattle /si'ætl/ 105
secateurs /'sekətɜːz/ 17
second /'sekənd/ 100
secondary school /'sekəndəri ˌskuːl/ 50, 53
second class /ˌsekənd 'klɑːs/ 65
second class post /ˌsekənd klɑːs 'pəʊst/ 76
second floor /ˌsekənd 'flɔːr/ 18
secretary /'sekrɪtəri/ 23
security /sɪ'kjʊərəti/ 70
seeds /siːdz/ 17
seed trays /'siːd treɪz/ 17
seesaw /'siːsɔː/ 51
sellotape™ /'seləteɪp/ 24, 77
semi-detached house /ˌsemidɪtætʃt 'haʊs/ 7
semi-skimmed milk /ˌsemi skɪmd 'mɪlk/ 64
send a fax /ˌsend ə 'fæks/ 25
send an e-mail /ˌsend ən 'iːmeɪl/ 25
senior school /'siːniə skuːl/ 50
September /sep'tembər/ 102
server /'sɜːvər/ 110
serviette /ˌsɜːvi'et/ 13
serving dish /'sɜːvɪŋ dɪʃ/ 13
set-square /'set skweər/ 52
settee /se'tiː/ 12
seven /'sevən/ 100
seven (o'clock) /ˌsevən ə'klɒk/ 103
seventeen /ˌsevən'tiːn/ 100
seventy /'sevənti/ 100
sew /səʊ/ 19
sewing /'səʊɪŋ/ 88
sewing basket /'səʊɪŋ ˌbɑːskɪt/ 48

sewing machine /'səʊɪŋ məˌʃiːn/ 48, 88
sex /seks/ 4
shade /ʃeɪd/ 91
shake hands /ˌʃeɪk 'hændz/ 34
shallow /'ʃæləʊ/ 114
shampoo /ʃæm'puː/ 10, 36, 37
shapes /ʃeɪps/ 46
shark /ʃɑːk/ 97
shave /ʃeɪv/ 6
shaved hair /ˌʃeɪvd heər/ 33
shaving brush /'ʃeɪvɪŋ brʌʃ/ 10
shaving gel /'ʃeɪvɪŋ dʒel/ 10, 37
shears /ʃɪəz/ 17
sheep /ʃiːp/ 95
sheet /ʃiːt/ 11
sheet music /'ʃiːt ˌmjuːzɪk/ 87
Sheffield /'ʃefiːld/ 104
shelf /ʃelf/ 10
shell /ʃel/ 91
shelves /ʃelvz/ 54
shepherd's pie with vegetables /ˌʃepədz paɪ wɪð 'vedʒtəbəlz/ 64
Shetland Islands /'ʃetlənd ˌaɪləndz/ 104
shin /ʃɪn/ 31
ship /ʃɪp/ 72
ships /ʃɪps/ 72
shirt /ʃɜːt/ 45
shoelace /'ʃuːleɪs/ 46
shoes /ʃuːz/ 43
shoe shop /'ʃuː ʃɒp/ 78
shop /ʃɒp/ 75
shopper /'ʃɒpər/ 57
shopping /'ʃɒpɪŋ/ 57
shopping bag /'ʃɒpɪŋ bæg/ 49, 57
short /ʃɔːt/ 33, 114
short hair /ˌ. '.'./ 33
shorts /ʃɔːts/ 44
short-sleeved /ˌʃɔːt 'sliːvd/ 46
shoulder /'ʃəʊldər/ 31
shoulder bag /'.. ˌ./ 49
shoulder-length hair /ˌ... '.'./ 33
shovel /'ʃʌvəl/ 28
shower /'ʃaʊər/ 10
shower curtain /'ʃaʊə ˌkɜːtn/ 10
shower gel /'ʃaʊə dʒel/ 10
shrimp /ʃrɪmp/ 97
shutter /'ʃʌtər/ 7
shuttlecock /'ʃʌtlkɒk/ 82
shy /ʃaɪ/ 113
side /saɪd/ 101
sideburns /'saɪdbɜːnz/ 33
sidelight /'saɪdlaɪt/ 67
side salad /'saɪd ˌsæləd/ 60
side table /'. ˌ../ 13
side vegetables /'saɪd ˌvedʒtəbəlz/ 60
sieve /sɪv/ 9
sign a letter /ˌsaɪn ə 'letər/ 25
signpost /'saɪnpəʊst/ 92
signs /saɪnz/ 69
silk /sɪlk/ 48
silver /'sɪlvər/ 49
sing /sɪŋ/ 34

singer /'sɪŋər/ **87**
single /'sɪŋgəl/ **4**
single bed /ˌsɪŋgəl 'bed/ **11**
single parent /ˌsɪŋgəl 'peərənt/ **5**
sink /sɪŋk/ **8**
sister /'sɪstər/ **5**
sister-in-law /'sɪstər ɪn ˌlɔː/ **5**
sit /sɪt/ **34**
sitting room /'sɪtɪŋ ruːm/ **18**
six /sɪks/ **100**
six-pack /'sɪks pæk/ **62**
sixteen /ˌsɪk'stiːn/ **100**
sixth form /'sɪksθ fɔːm/ **50**
sixty /'sɪksti/ **100**
skate /skeɪt/ **85**
skateboard /'skeɪtbɔːd/ **51**
skeleton /'skelɪtən/ **32**
ski /skiː/ **85**
ski boot /'skiː buːt/ **85**
skier /'skiːər/ **85**
skip /skɪp/ **86**
skipping rope /'skɪpɪŋ rəʊp/ **86**
skirt /skɜːt/ **44**
skull /skʌl/ **32**
sky /skaɪ/ **75**
sky-diver /'skaɪˌdaɪvər/ **83**
skydiving /'skaɪˌdaɪvɪŋ/ **83**
skyline /'skaɪlaɪn/ **75**
skyscraper /'skaɪˌskreɪpər/ **75**
sledge /sledʒ/ **85**
sledgehammer /'sledʒˌhæmər/ **28**
sledging /'sledʒɪŋ/ **85**
sleep /sliːp/ **6**
sleeping bag /'sliːpɪŋ bæg/ **92**
sleeve /sliːv/ **46**
slice /slaɪs/ **63**
slide /slaɪd/ **51, 112**
slide projector /'slaɪd prəˌdʒektər/ **112**
slim /slɪm/ **33**
sling /slɪŋ/ **41**
slip road /'slɪp rəʊd/ **68**
slippers /'slɪpəz/ **43**
slippery road sign /ˌslɪpəri 'rəʊd saɪn/ **69**
slot /slɒt/ **79**
slow /sləʊ/ **114**
slug pellets /'slʌg ˌpeləts/ **17**
small animals /ˌsmɔːl 'ænɪməlz / **99**
small intestine /ˌsmɔːl ɪn'testɪn/ **32**
smile /smaɪl/ **34**
smoked ham /ˌsməʊkt 'hæm/ **59**
smoked salmon /ˌsməʊkt 'sæmən/ **60**
smooth /smuːð/ **114**
snail /sneɪl/ **99**
snake /sneɪk/ **96**
snapdragon /'snæpˌdrægən/ **16**
snorkel /'snɔːkəl/ **84**
snorkeller /'snɔːkələr/ **84**
snorkelling /'snɔːkəlɪŋ/ **84**
snout /snaʊt/ **97**
snowboard /'snəʊbɔːd/ **85**
snowmobile /'snəʊməˌbiːl/ **85**

snowmobiling /'snəʊməˌbiːlɪŋ/ **85**
snowy /'snəʊi/ **107**
soap /səʊp/ **10**
soap dish /'səʊp dɪʃ/ **10**
soap dispenser /'səʊp dɪˌspensər/ **10**
sociology /ˌsəʊsi'ɒlədʒi, ˌsəʊʃi-/ **53**
socket /'sɒkɪt/ **15**
socks /sɒks/ **44, 45**
sofa /'səʊfə/ **12**
soft /sɒft/ **114**
soft top /'sɒft tɒp/ **67**
soft toy /ˌsɒft 'tɔɪ/ **14**
software /'sɒftweər/ **109**
solar system /'səʊlə ˌsɪstəm/ **108**
soldier /'səʊldʒər/ **21**
sole /səʊl/ **46**
solicitor /sə'lɪsɪtər/ **30**
son /sʌn/ **5**
son-in-law /'sʌn ɪn lɔː/ **5**
sore throat /ˌsɔː 'θrəʊt/ **38**
soup /suːp/ **57, 64**
soup spoon /'suːp spuːn/ **13**
South Carolina /ˌsaʊθ kærə'laɪnə/ **105**
South Dakota /ˌsaʊθ də'kəʊtə/ **105**
space shuttle /'speɪs ˌʃʌtl/ **108**
space suit /'speɪs suːt/ **108**
spade /speɪd/ **17, 91**
spaghetti bolognese /spəˌgeti bɒlə'neɪz/ **64**
Spanish /'spænɪʃ/ **53**
speak /spiːk/ **34**
speaker /'spiːkər/ **111**
Special Delivery /ˌspeʃəl dɪ'lɪvəri/ **76**
speed skater /'spiːd ˌskeɪtər/ **85**
speed skating /'spiːd ˌskeɪtɪŋ/ **85**
speedometer /spɪ'dɒmɪtər/ **67**
sphere /sfɪər/ **101**
spice rack /'spaɪs ræk/ **8**
spices /'spaɪsɪz/ **8, 58**
spider /'spaɪdər/ **99**
spinach /'spɪnɪdʒ, -ɪtʃ/ **55**
spine /spaɪn/ **32**
spines /spaɪnz/ **99**
spinning /'spɪnɪŋ/ **88**
spiral /'spaɪərəl/ **101**
spirit level /'spɪrɪt ˌlevəl/ **28**
sponge mop /'spʌndʒ mɒp/ **15**
sports car /'spɔːts kɑːr/ **66**
sports shop /'spɔːts ʃɒp/ **78**
sportswear /'spɔːtsweər/ **45**
spotlight /'spɒtlaɪt/ **87**
spots /spɒts/ **96**
spotted /'spɒtɪd/ **47**
spreadsheet /'spredʃiːt/ **109**
spring /sprɪŋ/ **107**
spring onion /sprɪŋ 'ʌnjən/ **55**
sprinkler /'sprɪŋklər/ **17**
square /skweər/ **26, 101**
squash /skwɒʃ/ **82**
squash ball /'. ./ **82**
squash player /'. ,../ **82**

squash racket /'skwɒʃ ˌrækɪt/ **82**
stadium /'steɪdiəm/ **80**
stage /steɪdʒ/ **87**
stage set /'steɪdʒ set/ **87**
stain /steɪn/ **48**
stair cupboard /'steə ˌkʌbəd/ **18**
stairs /steəz/ **18**
stamp /stæmp/ **76**
stamp album /'stæmp ˌælbəm/ **88**
stamp collecting /'stæmp kəˌlektɪŋ/ **88**
stamp machine /'stæmp məˌʃiːn/ **76**
stand /stænd/ **34, 80**
Stanley knife™ /'stænli naɪf/ **26**
staple /'steɪpəl/ **25**
stapler /'steɪplər/ **24**
star /stɑːr/ **108**
starfish /'stɑːˌfɪʃ/ **97**
starfruit /'stɑːˌfruːt/ **56**
starters /'stɑːtəz/ **60**
state school /'steɪt skuːl/ **50**
stately home /ˌsteɪtli 'həʊm/ **93**
stationer's /'steɪʃənəz/ **78**
stationery /'steɪʃənəri/ **77**
steak /steɪk/ **59**
steam /stiːm/ **63**
steamer /'stiːmər/ **9**
steep hill sign /stiːp 'hɪl saɪn/ **69**
steering wheel /'stɪərɪŋ wiːl/ **67**
stepbrother /'stepbrʌðər/ **5**
stepdaughter /'stepdɔːtər/ **5**
stepfather /'stepfɑːðər/ **5**
stepmother /'stepmʌðər/ **5**
stepsister /'stepsɪstər/ **5**
stepson /'stepsʌn/ **5**
stereo system /'steriəʊ ˌsɪstəm/ **111**
steriliser /'sterɪlaɪzər/ **14**
stern /stɜːn/ **72**
stethoscope /'steθəskəʊp/ **40**
stewing beef /'stjuːɪŋ biːf/ **59**
sticking plaster /'stɪkɪŋ ˌplɑːstər/ **39**
sticky tape /'stɪki teɪp/ **77**
stile /staɪl/ **92**
still camera /'stɪl ˌkæmərə/ **112**
still mineral water /stɪl 'mɪnərəl ˌwɔːtər/ **60**
stir /stɜːr/ **35, 63**
stir fry /'stɜː fraɪ/ **63**
stirrup /'stɪrəp/ **83**
stitches /'stɪtʃɪz/ **41**
stockings /'stɒkɪŋz/ **44**
stomach /'stʌmək/ **31, 32**
stomachache /'stʌmək-eɪk/ **38, 39**
stop sign /'stɒp saɪn/ **69**
storage jar /'stɔːrɪdʒ dʒɑːr/ **8**
stork /stɔːk/ **98**
stormy /'stɔːmi/ **107**
straight /streɪt/ **101**
straight hair /ˌstreɪt 'heər/ **33**
straw /strɔː/ **61**

strawberry /'strɔːbəri/ **56**
stream /striːm/ **106**
street /striːt/ **74**
streetlight /'striːtlaɪt/ **68, 75**
street map /'striːt mæp/ **77**
stretch /stretʃ/ **86**
stretcher /'stretʃər/ **79**
string /strɪŋ/ **76, 77**
strings /strɪŋz/ **90**
striped /straɪpt/ **47**
stripes /straɪps/ **96**
stub /stʌb/ **73**
stubble /'stʌbəl/ **33**
student welfare office /ˌstjuːdənt 'welfeər ˌɒfɪs/ **54**
study /'stʌdi/ **19**
stuffed peppers /ˌstʌft 'pepəz/ **60**
stump /stʌmp/ **80**
St Valentine's Day /sənt 'væləntaɪnz ˌdeɪ/ **102**
style /staɪl/ **36**
styling brush /'staɪlɪŋ brʌʃ/ **36**
styling mousse /'staɪlɪŋ muːs/ **36**
sugar /'ʃʊgər/ **58**
suit /suːt/ **44, 45**
suitcase /'suːtkeɪs/ **29, 70**
summer /'sʌmər/ **107**
sun /sʌn/ **108**
sunbather /'sʌnbeɪðər/ **91**
sunburn /'sʌnbɜːn/ **38**
Sunday /'sʌndi/ **102**
sunfish /'sʌnˌfɪʃ/ **97**
sunglasses /'sʌnˌglɑːsɪz/ **91**
sun lounger /'sʌn ˌlaʊndʒər/ **16**
sunny /'sʌni/ **107**
sunscreen /'sʌnskriːn/ **91**
surfboard /'sɜːfbɔːd/ **84, 91**
surfer /'sɜːfər/ **84, 91**
surfing and wind-surfing /ˌsɜːfɪŋ ənd 'wɪnd sɜːfɪŋ/ **84**
surgeon /'sɜːdʒən/ **41**
surgical collar /'sɜːdʒɪkəl ˈkɒlər/ **41**
surgical gloves /'sɜːdʒɪkəl ˌglʌvz/ **41**
surname /'sɜːneɪm/ **4**
surprised /sə'praɪzd/ **113**
suspect /'sʌspekt/ **30**
suspicious /sə'spɪʃəs/ **113**
swallow /'swɒləʊ/ **98**
swan /swɒn/ **98**
sweater /'swetər/ **43**
sweaters /'swetəz/ **43**
sweatshirt /'swet-ʃɜːt/ **44**
swede /swiːd/ **55**
sweep /swiːp/ **19**
sweetcorn /'swiːtkɔːn/ **55, 57**
sweets /swiːts/ **61**
sweet shop /'swiːt ʃɒp/ **78**
Swiftair™ /'swɪfteər/ **76**
swimmer /'swɪmər/ **84**
swimming /'swɪmɪŋ/ **84**
swimming costume /'swɪmɪŋ ˌkɒstjʊm/ **45, 91**
swimming hat/cap /'swɪmɪŋ hæt, 'swɪmɪŋ kæp/ **84**

swimming pool /'swimiŋ puːl/ 84

swimming trunks /'swimiŋ trʌŋks/ 45, 91

swimsuit /'swimsuːt/ 45

swing /swiŋ/ 16

swings /swiŋz/ 51

Swiss cheese /ˌswis 'tʃiːz/ 59

swivel chair /'swivəl tʃeər/ 24

symphony orchestra /'simfəni ˌɔːkistrə/ 87

syringe /sə'rindʒ/ 41

table /'teibəl/ 109

tablespoonful /'teibəlspuːnfʊl/ 62

table tennis /'.. ˌ../ 82

tail /teil/ 71, 94, 97, 98

tailor /'teilər/ 48

take /teik/ 35

take notes /teik 'nəʊts/ 25

take-off /'. ./ 71

take the bus to school /teik ðə ˌbʌs tə 'skuːl / 19

take the children to school /teik ðə ˌtʃildrən tə 'skuːl/ 19

talk /tɔːk/ 34

tall /tɔːl/ 33

tangerine /ˌtændʒə'riːn/ 56

tap /tæp/ 8, 17

tape deck /'teip dek/ 111

tape measure /'teip ˌmeʒər/ 26, 48

tape recorder /'teip riˌkɔːdər/ 111

taramasalata /ˌtærəməsə'lɑːtə/ 59

target /'tɑːgit/ 83

tartan /'tɑːtn/ 47

taxi /'tæksi/ 65

taxi driver /'tæksi ˌdraivər/ 21, 65

tea /tiː/ 58, 60, 64

teacher /'tiːtʃər/ 22, 52

teapot /'tiːpɒt/ 13

tear /tiər/ 35, 48

teaspoon /'tiːspuːn/ 13

teaspoonful /'tiːspuːnfʊl/ 62

teat /tiːt/ 14

tea towel /'tiː ˌtaʊəl/ 8

technology in the classroom /tekˌnɒlədʒi in ðə 'klɑːsruːm/ 52

teddy bear /'tedi beər/ 14

teenager /'tiːneidʒər/ 4

telemarketing executive /ˌteli'mɑːkitiŋ igˌzekjʊtiv/ 23

telephone /'telifəʊn/ 24, 112

telephone box /'... ˌ./ 79

telephone number /'telifəʊn ˌnʌmbər/ 4, 20

telescope /'teliskəʊp/ 88

television/TV /ˌtelə'viʒən, ˌtiː 'viː/ 12, 111

temperature /'tempərətʃər/ 38, 39, 107

temperature gauge /'tempərətʃə ˌgeidʒ/ 67

temple /'tempəl/ 32

ten /ten/ 100

ten pence/ten pence piece /ˌten 'pens, ˌten pens 'piːs/ 73

ten percent /ˌten pə'sent/ 100

ten pounds/ten pound note /ˌten 'paʊndz, ˌten paʊnd 'nəʊt/ 73

ten thousand /ˌten 'θaʊzənd/ 100

Tennessee /ˌtenə'siː/ 105

tennis /'tenis/ 82

tennis ball /'.. ./ 82

tennis player /'.. ˌ../ 82

tennis racket /'tenis ˌrækit/ 82

tent /tent/ 92

tentacle /'tentəkəl/ 97

terraced houses /ˌterəst 'haʊziz/ 7

test tubes /'test tjuːbz/ 52

Texas /'teksəs/ 105

textbook /'tekstbʊk/ 52

theatre /'θiətər/ 87

the gym /ðə 'dʒim/ 52

theme park /'θiːm pɑːk/ 93

the planets /ðə 'plænits/ 108

therapist /'θerəpist/ 40

thermometer /θə'mɒmitər/ 39, 107

the runway /ðə 'rʌnwei/ 71

the science lab /ðə 'saiəns læb/ 52

the terminal /ðə 'tɜːminəl/ 70

the underground /ði 'ʌndəgraʊnd/ 65

thick /θik/ 114

thigh /θai/ 31

thimble /'θimbəl/ 48

thin /θin/ 114

third /θɜːd/ 100

thirteen /ˌθɜː'tiːn/ 100

thirteen hundred hours /ˌθɜːtiːn 'hʌndrəd ˌaʊəz/ 103

thirty /'θɜːti/ 100

thread /θred/ 48

three /θriː/ 100

three quarters /θriː 'kwɔːtəz/ 62

three-star hotel /ˌθriː stɑː həʊ'tel/ 29

throat /θrəʊt/ 32

throat lozenges /'θrəʊt ˌlɒzindʒiz/ 39

through /θruː/ 116

throw /θrəʊ/ 86

thumb /θʌm/ 31

Thursday /'θɜːzdi/ 102

ticket /'tikit/ 70

tidy /'taidi/ 114

tie /tai/ 45

tie clip /'tai klip/ 49

tie up a branch /ˌtai ʌp ə 'brɑːntʃ/ 17

tiger /'taigər/ 96

tight /tait/ 46, 114

tights /taits/ 44

tile /tail/ 10

time card /'taim kɑːd/ 27

time clock /'taim klɒk/ 27

timetable /'taimˌteibəl/ 65

tin /tin/ 62

tinned food /ˌtind 'fuːd/ 57

tin opener /'tin ˌəʊpənər/ 9

tissues /'tiʃuːz/ 39

to /tuː/ 115

toad /təʊd/ 99

toast /təʊst/ 64

toaster /'təʊstər/ 9

toddler /'tɒdlər/ 4, 51

toe /təʊ/ 31

toilet /'tɔilit/ 10, 18

toiletries /'tɔilitriz/ 37

toilet roll /'tɔilit rəʊl/ 10

tomato /tə'mɑːtəʊ‖-'meitəʊ/ 55

tomato ketchup /.ˌ.. '../ 61

tomato soup /.ˌ.. './ 60

tongs /tɒŋz/ 52

tongue /tʌŋ/ 32

toolbar /'tuːlbɑːr/ 109

tool belt /'tuːl belt/ 28

toolbox /'tuːlbɒks/ 26

tooth /tuːθ/ 32, 42

toothache /'tuːθ-eik/ 38

toothbrush /'tuːθbrʌʃ/ 10, 42

toothbrush holder /'tuːθbrʌʃ ˌhəʊldər/ 10

toothpaste /'tuːθpeist/ 10, 42

toothpick /'tuːθpik/ 42

top /tɒp/ 44, 101

topaz /'təʊpæz/ 49

topic /'tɒpik/ 110

torch /tɔːtʃ/ 112

tortoise /'tɔːtəs/ 96

touch /tʌtʃ/ 34

tour guide /'tʊə gaid/ 93

tourist /'tʊərist/ 93

towards /tə'wɔːdz/ 116

towel /'taʊəl/ 36

towel dry /'taʊəl drai/ 36

towel rail /'taʊəl reil/ 10

tower block /'taʊə blɒk/ 75

towrope /'təʊrəʊp/ 84

toy /tɔi/ 51

toy shop /'tɔi ʃɒp/ 78

track /træk/ 65, 85

tracksuit /'træksuːt/ 45

tractor /'træktər/ 66

traffic /'træfik/ 74

traffic cone /'træfik kəʊn/ 69

traffic lights /'træfik laits/ 68, 74

trailer /'treilər/ 71

train /trein/ 65

trainers /'treinəz/ 45

travel agency /'trævəl ˌeidʒənsi/ 78

travel agent /'trævəl ˌeidʒənt/ 23

traveller's cheque /'trævələz tʃek/ 73

tray /trei/ 13, 71

treadmill /'tredˌmil/ 86

tree /triː/ 16

tricycle /'traisikəl/ 51

trolley /'trɒli/ 57

trombone /trɒm'bəʊn/ 90

tropical fish /ˌtrɒpikəl 'fiʃ/ 94

trouser press /'traʊzə pres/ 29

trousers /'traʊzəz/ 44, 45

trout /traʊt/ 97

trowel /'traʊəl/ 17, 28

truck AmE /trʌk/ 66

trumpet /'trʌmpit/ 90

trunk /trʌŋk/ 96

trunks /trʌŋks/ 81

T-shirt /'tiː ʃɜːt/ 44, 45

tub /tʌb/ 12, 17, 62

tuba /'tjuːbə/ 90

tube /tjuːb/ 62

tube of glue /ˌ.. './ 77

Tuesday /'tjuːzdi/ 102

tulip /'tjuːlip/ 16

tumble dryer /'tʌmbəl ˌdraiər/ 15

tuna /'tjuːnə/ 57

tuner /'tjuːnər/ 111

tunnel /'tʌnl/ 65

turkey /'tɜːki/ 59, 95

turnip /'tɜːnip/ 55

turquoise /'tɜːkwɔiz/ 47

turtle /'tɜːtl/ 97

tusk /tʌsk/ 96, 97

tutor /'tjuːtər/ 54

tutorial /tjuː'tɔːriəl/ 54

tuxedo /tʌk'siːdəʊ/ 45

TV aerial /ˌtiː 'viː ˌeəriəl/ 7

tweezers /'twiːzəz/ 37

twelve /twelv/ 100

twelve hundred hours /twelv 'hʌndrəd aʊəz/ 103

twelve o'clock (midnight) /ˌtwelv ə'klɒk, 'midnait/ 103

twelve o'clock (noon/midday) /ˌtwelv ə'klɒk, nuːn, mid'dei/ 103

twenty /'twenti/ 100

twenty-four hundred hours /ˌtwenti fɔː 'hʌndrəd ˌaʊəz / 103

twenty-one /ˌ.. '. / 100

twenty pence/twenty pence piece /ˌtwenti 'pens, ˌtwenti pens 'piːs/ 73

twenty percent /ˌtwenti pə'sent/ 100

twenty pounds/twenty pound note /ˌtwenti 'paʊndz, ˌtwenti paʊnd 'nəʊt/ 73

twin room /'twin ruːm/ 29

two /tuː/ 100

two pence/two pence piece /tuː 'pens, ˌtuː pens 'piːs/ 73

two pounds/two pound coin /tuː 'paʊndz, ˌtuː paʊnd 'kɔin/ 73

two-way radio /ˌtuː wei 'reidiəʊ/ 28

two-wheeled vehicles /ˌtuː wiːld 'viːikəlz/ 66

type a letter /ˌtaip ə 'letər/ 25

tyre /taiər/ 67

umbrella /ʌm'brelə/ 16, 43

umpire /'ʌmpaiər/ 80

uncle and nephew /ˌʌnkəl ənd 'nefjuː/ 5

under /'ʌndər/ 115

underneath /ˌʌndəˈniːθ/ **116**
underground entrance
/ˌʌndəɡraʊnd ˈentrəns/ **75**
underpants /ˈʌndəpænts/ **45**
undershirt /ˈʌndəʃɜːt/ **45**
underwear /ˈʌndəweər/ **44, 45**
university /ˌjuːnɪˈvɜːsəti/ **50**
university degrees
/ˌjuːnɪvɜːsəti dɪˈɡriːz/ **50**
university graduate
/ˌjuːnɪvɜːsəti ˈɡrædʒuət/ **50**
untidy /ʌnˈtaɪdi/ **114**
up /ʌp/ **115**
upper arm /ˈʌpər ɑːm/ **31**
upstairs /ˌʌpˈsteəz/ **18**
Uranus /ˈjʊərənəs, jʊˈreɪnəs/
108
Utah /ˈjuːtɑː/ **105**
utility room /juːˈtɪləti ruːm/
18

vacuum /ˈvækjuəm/ **19**
vacuum cleaner
/ˈvækjuəm ˌkliːnər/ **15**
valance /ˈvæləns/ **11**
valley /ˈvæli/ **106**
van /væn/ **66**
vase /vɑːz‖veɪs/ **12**
VCR /ˌviː siː ˈɑːr/ **111**
vegetable garden
/ˈvedʒtəbəl ˌɡɑːdn/ **16**
vein /veɪn/ **32**
Velcro™ /ˈvelkrəʊ/ **48**
Venus /ˈviːnəs/ **108**
verdict /ˈvɜːdɪkt/ **30**
Vermont /vəˈmɒnt/ **105**
vest /vest/ **45**
vet /vet/ **22**
veterinarian *AmE*
/ˌvetərɪˈneəriən/ **22**
vice /vaɪs/ **26**
video camera
/ˈvɪdiəʊ ˌkæmərə/ **112**
video cassette /ˈvɪdiəʊ kəˌset/
111
video cassette recorder
/ˌvɪdiəʊ kəˈset rɪˌkɔːdər/
111
video games /ˈvɪdiəʊ ɡeɪmz/
89
video recorder
/ˈvɪdiəʊ rɪˌkɔːdər/ **12, 52**
video shop /ˈvɪdiəʊ ʃɒp/ **78**
village /ˈvɪlɪdʒ/ **93**
vinegar /ˈvɪnɪɡər/ **58, 61**
viola /viˈəʊlə/ **90**
violin /ˌvaɪəˈlɪn/ **90**
Virginia /vəˈdʒɪniə/ **105**
V-neck jumper
/ˌviː nek ˈdʒʌmpər/ **43**
vocalist /ˈvəʊkəlɪst/ **87**

volleyball /ˈvɒlibɔːl/ **81**
volleyball player /ˈ... ˌ../ **81**

waist /weɪst/ **31**
waistband /ˈweɪstbænd/ **46**
waistcoat /ˈweɪskəʊt, ˈweskət/
45
waiter /ˈweɪtər/ **21, 60**
waiting room /ˈweɪtɪŋ ruːm/
41
wake up /weɪk ˈʌp/ **6**
Wales /weɪlz/ **104**
walk /wɔːk/ **86**
walking boot /ˈwɔːkɪŋ buːt/
43, 92
Walkman /ˈwɔːkmən/ **111**
walk the dog /ˌ.. ˈ./ **19**
wall /wɔːl/ **18**
wall bars /ˈwɔːl bɑːz/ **52**
wall chart /ˈwɔːl tʃɑːt/ **52**
wallet /ˈwɒlɪt/ **49**
wallpaper /ˈwɔːlˌpeɪpər/ **11**
walnut /ˈwɔːlnʌt/ **56**
walrus /ˈwɔːlrəs/ **97**
wardrobe /ˈwɔːdrəʊb/ **11**
warehouse /ˈweəhaʊs/ **27**
warm /wɔːm/ **107**
wash /wɒʃ/ **36, 63**
wash the dishes /ˌ.. ˈ../ **19**
wash the floor /ˌ.. ˈ./ **19**
washbasin /ˈwɒʃˌbeɪsən/ **10, 36**
washer /ˈwɒʃər/ **26**
washing line /ˈwɒʃɪŋ laɪn/ **15**
washing machine
/ˈwɒʃɪŋ məˌʃiːn/ **15**
washing powder
/ˈwɒʃɪŋ ˌpaʊdər/ **15, 58**
Washington /ˈwɒʃɪŋtən/ **105**
Washington, DC
/ˌwɒʃɪŋtən ˌdiː ˈsiː/ **105**
washing-up liquid
/ˌwɒʃɪŋ ˈʌp ˌlɪkwɪd/ **19**
wash your face /ˌwɒʃ jɔː ˈfeɪs/
6
wasp /wɒsp/ **99**
wasp nest /ˈ. ˈ./ **99**
wastepaper basket
/ˈweɪstˌpeɪpə ˌbɑːskɪt/ **24**
watch /wɒtʃ/ **49**
watch (TV) /ˌwɒtʃ tiː ˈviː/ **6**
water /ˈwɔːtər/ **79**
waterfall /ˈwɔːtəfɔːl/ **106**
watering can /ˈwɔːtərɪŋ ˌkæn/
17
watermelon /ˈwɔːtəˌmelən/ **56**
water ski /ˈ.. ./ **84**
water skier /ˈ.. ˌ../ **84**
water skiing /ˈwɔːtə ˌskiːɪŋ/
84
water the plants /ˌ.. ˈ./ **17**

wave /weɪv/ **34, 91**
wavy hair /ˌweɪvi ˈheər/ **33**
weather /ˈweðər/ **107**
web /web/ **99**
web address
/ˈweb əˌdres‖ˌædres/ **110**
web browser /ˈweb ˌbraʊzər/
110
website /ˈwebsaɪt/ **110**
Wednesday /ˈwenzdi/ **102**
weed the flowerbed
/ˌwiːd ðə ˈflaʊəbed/ **17**
weigh /weɪ/ **63**
weights /weɪts/ **86**
West Virginia /ˌwest vəˈdʒɪniə/
105
wet /wet/ **114**
wet suit /ˈ. ./ **84**
whale /weɪl/ **97**
wheel /wiːl/ **67, 83**
wheelbarrow /ˈwiːlˌbærəʊ/ **17, 28**
wheelchair /ˈwiːltʃeər/ **41**
whisk /wɪsk/ **9**
whiskers /ˈwɪskəz/ **94**
white /waɪt/ **47**
whiteboard /ˈwaɪtbɔːd/ **52**
whiteboard marker
/ˈwaɪtbɔːd ˌmɑːkər/ **52**
white bread /ˌ. ˈ./ **59**
white-collar worker /ˌ. ˈ.. ˌ../
23
white wine /ˌwaɪt ˈwaɪn/ **58, 60**
wholemeal bread
/ˌhəʊlmiːl ˈbred/ **59**
whole trout /ˌhəʊl ˈtraʊt/ **59**
wicket /ˈwɪkɪt/ **80**
wicket keeper /ˈwɪkɪt ˌkiːpər/
80
wide /waɪd/ **46, 114**
widow /ˈwɪdəʊ/ **4**
widower /ˈwɪdəʊər/ **4**
width /wɪdθ/ **101**
wife /waɪf/ **5**
wildlife park /ˈwaɪldlaɪf ˌpɑːk/
93
windbreak /ˈwɪndbreɪk/ **91**
window /ˈwɪndəʊ/ **7, 12, 18, 71, 109**
window cleaner
/ˈwɪndəʊ ˌkliːnər/ **21**
window seat /ˈwɪndəʊ siːt/ **71**
windscreen wiper
/ˈwɪndskriːn ˌwaɪpər/ **67**
wind-surfer /ˈwɪnd ˌsɜːfər/ **84**
windy /ˈwɪndi/ **107**
wine glass /ˈwaɪn ɡlɑːs/ **13**
wine list /ˈwaɪn lɪst/ **60**
wing /wɪŋ/ **67, 71**
wing mirror /ˈwɪŋ ˌmɪrər/ **67**

wings /wɪŋz/ **98**
winter /ˈwɪntər/ **107**
Wisconsin /wɪˈskɒnsɪn/ **105**
withdrawal slip /wɪðˈdrɔːəl
slɪp/ **73**
witness /ˈwɪtnɪs/ **30**
wok /wɒk/ **9**
woman /ˈwʊmən/ **4**
wood /wʊd/ **106**
woodwind /ˈwʊdˌwɪnd/ **90**
woodworking /ˈwʊdˌwɜːkɪŋ/
88
wool /wʊl/ **48**
word processor
/ˈwɜːd ˈprəʊsesər/ **109**
workbench /ˈwɜːkbentʃ/ **26**
worker /ˈwɜːkər/ **27**
work station /ˈwɜːk ˌsteɪʃən/
27
work-surface /ˈwɜːk ˌsɜːfɪs/ **8**
worktop /ˈwɜːktɒp/ **8**
World Wide Web
/ˌwɜːld waɪd ˈweb/ **110**
wrapping paper
/ˈræpɪŋ ˌpeɪpər/ **77**
wrench /rentʃ/ **26**
wrestler /ˈreslər/ **82**
wrestling /ˈreslɪŋ/ **82**
wrist /rɪst/ **31**
write /raɪt/ **35**
write a memo /ˌraɪt ə ˈmeməʊ/
25
writing paper /ˈraɪtɪŋ ˌpeɪpər/
77
writing table /ˈraɪtɪŋ ˌteɪbəl/
12
Wyoming /waɪˈəʊmɪŋ/ **105**

X-ray /ˈeks reɪ/ **40**
X-rays /ˈeks reɪz/ **41**
X-ray scanner
/ˈeks reɪ ˌskænər/ **70**
xylophone /ˈzaɪləfəʊn/ **90**

yacht /jɒt/ **72**
yard *AmE* /jɑːd/ **7**
year /jɪər/ **102**
yellow /ˈjeləʊ/ **47**
yoghurt/yogurt /ˈjɒɡət/ **57**
York /jɔːk/ **104**

zebra /ˈzebrə, ˈziː-/ **96**
zebra crossing /ˌzebrə ˈkrɒsɪŋ/
68, 74
zip /zɪp/ **46**
zip drive /ˈzɪp draɪv/ **109**
zoo /zuː/ **93**

EXERCISES

1 PEOPLE

1.1 What do you do in the morning? Put the verbs in order.

get up   dry yourself   1. _____   4. _____

have a shower   get dressed   2. _____   5. _____

wake up   go to work   3. _____   6. _____

1.2 Use the information about Brad Pitt to complete the application form.

Brad Pitt   18/12/1963   994-9872

1106 Hollywood Drive, Los Angeles   Actor   Male

CA 98554   Married   American

Jennifer Aniston   No children   Shawnee, Oklahoma

1. First name _____   8. Nationality _____

2. Surname _____   9. Date of birth _____

3. Sex _____   10. Place of birth _____

4. Occupation _____   11. Marital status _____

5. Address _____   12. Husband's/wife's name _____

6. Postcode _____   13. Number of children _____

7. Telephone number _____

1.3 Put the male and female equivalents in the correct column.

granddaughter, sister, nephew, half-sister, father, aunt, grandmother, mother-in-law, stepfather, stepson

	Male	Female	Male	Female
Example	widower	widow		
1.	brother	_____	6. _____	stepdaughter
2.	_____	mother	7. father-in-law	_____
3.	uncle	_____	8. half-brother	_____
4.	grandfather	_____	9. grandson	_____
5.	_____	niece	10. stepmother	_____

1.4 Marital status. Write these words out correctly.

1. insleg _____   4. mrreiedar _____

2. riedram _____   5. vdecroid _____

3. idwwo _____

2 HOUSING

2.1 **Where in your house do you find these objects? Draw a line to link the objects to the correct rooms.**

washbasin   chest of drawers

oven | kitchen | coffee table

laundry basket | bathroom | settee/sofa

armchair | dining room | dining table

headboard | living room | napkin

quilt | bedroom | spice rack

washing-up liquid

2.2 **Choose the part of the house where we normally do these things.**

dining room, bedroom (2), bathroom (2), kitchen (2), garden (2)

Example   We usually watch the television in the <u>living room</u>.

1. We usually sleep in the _____
2. We eat our meals in the _____
3. We wash our hair in the _____
4. We cook a barbecue in the _____
5. We clean our teeth in the _____

6. We make dinner in the _____
7. We sit in the sun in the _____
8. We wash the dishes in the _____
9. We make the beds in the _____

2.3 **Write the name of the part of the house where you would find these items and cross out the object that is in the wrong place.**

oven	wardrobe	toilet	armchair	lawn
freezer	dressing table	toothbrush	dishcloth	pond
dishwasher	alarm clock	tile	magazine rack	bush
sink	bath	mirror	sofa	swing
fridge	lamp	quilt	bookcase	cot
~~swing~~	mattress	washbasin	coffee table	fence
				hedge

Example   kitchen   **1.** _____   **2.** _____   **3.** _____   **4.** _____

2.4 **Complete the words. All these things go on the dining room table.**

1. f_rk
2. sp_on
3. w_ne glas_
4. des_ertspo_n
5. ser_iette

6. kn_fe
7. so_p spo_n
8. s_lt
9. p_pper
10. t_asp_on

EXERCISES

3 WORK

3.1 Link the place of work to the job.

hospital, court, studio, restaurant, school, university, kitchen, office, bank

1. secretary _____

2. nurse _____

3. teacher _____

4. lecturer _____

5. judge _____

6. photographer _____

7. bank clerk _____

8. cook _____

9. waiter _____

3.2 Fill in the verbs to complete the word. All of the verbs are activities in the office.

	O			appointments
	F			papers
	F			refreshments
	I			a letter
			C		a document
	E			an e-mail

3.3 Match the pictures and the words. Put the correct number next to the word.

desk diary ❑	paper clip ❑	telephone ❑	in tray ❑
notepad ❑	hole-punch ❑	lamp ❑	typewriter ❑
pencil ❑	stapler ❑	calendar ❑	pen ❑
rubber ❑	Sellotape ❑	out tray ❑	filing cabinet ❑

4 THE BODY

4.1 Fill in the gaps to complete the physical description.
Each dash represents a letter.

This man has got _ _ _ _ _   _ _ _ _ hair. He has got _ _ _ eyes and a _ _ _ _ nose.

He has _ _ _ _ eyelashes and thick _ _ _ _ _ _ _ _ . His mouth is _ _ _ _ _ and

his _ _ _ _ are small too. He has a _ _ _ _ beard and a _ _ _ _ _ _ _ _ _ .

4.2 Write the verbs of movement under the correct picture.

to frown, to cry, to push, to pull, to sit, to talk, to sing, to hug, to shake hands, to wave

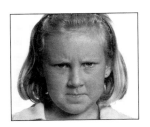    

1. _____   2. _____   3. _____   4. _____   5. _____

6. _____   7. _____   8. _____   9. _____   10. _____

4.3 Match the opposites.

1. tall   **2.** dark hair   **3.** overweight   **4.** straight hair   **5.** short hair

a) slim   **b)** long hair   **c)** short   **d)** fair hair   **e)** curly hair

4.4 Put these words in the correct box according to where they are on our bodies.

thigh, nose, wrist, hip, waist, palm, ankle, calf, knee, elbow, stomach, ears, forehead, kneecap, cheek, fingers, thumb, back, mouth, lips

Head/Face	Arm/Hand	Leg	Body
_____	_____	_____	_____
_____	_____	_____	_____
_____	_____	_____	_____
_____	_____	_____	
_____			

EXERCISES

5 FOOD

5.1 **Complete the restaurant dialogue with the words below.**

apple pie, carrots, prawn cocktail, roast beef with Yorkshire pudding, still mineral water, peas

WAITER Hello sir. What would you like to eat?

CUSTOMER For the starter I would like _____.

WAITER And for main course?

CUSTOMER I would like _____ and

some _____ and

_____ for side vegetables.

WAITER Would you like a dessert?

CUSTOMER Yes. Can I have _____ please?

WAITER And to drink?

CUSTOMER I would like _____ .

5.2 **Put these words in the correct boxes.**

chicken, orange juice, pepper, oil, bacon, minced beef, pork chops, sugar, cereal, vinegar, cod fillet, liver, salt, pasta, rice, lobster, crab, biscuits, beer, mineral water

Meat	Drinks	Fish and seafood	Dry goods and condiments	
_____	_____	_____	_____	_____
_____	_____	_____	_____	_____
_____	_____	_____	_____	_____
_____			_____	_____
_____			_____	

5.3 **Food word soup**

Look at these pictures. Find the words for these foods in the word soup.

```
D  O  U  G  H  N  U  T  G  E  W  O
S  W  E  E  T  S  A  R  D  I  U  P
C  R  I  S  P  S  K  P  U  V  X  E
O  O  B  H  I  A  G  L  K  S  T  A
N  T  L  W  Z  A  R  O  Y  I  M  N
E  R  P  A  Z  C  E  F  G  K  N  U
G  U  L  S  A  N  D  W  I  C  H  T
N  H  A  M  B  U  R  G  E  R  A  R
```

6 TRANSPORT

6.1 Use the words in the box to finish the sentences below.

clock, train station, ticket collector, platform, track, luggage compartment, bus stop, timetable

1. You should never walk on the _____
2. You wait for the train on the _____
3. You can leave your bags in a _____
4. You wait for a bus at the _____
5. To know what time the train leaves look at the _____
6. To know the time in the station look at the _____
7. You have to show your ticket to a _____
8. The train arrives in the _____

6.2 Number the words.

roof-rack ☐   bumper ☐   bonnet ☐   windscreen wiper ☐   exhaust pipe ☐   wing mirror ☐

headlight ☐   indicator ☐   numberplate ☐   petrol cap ☐   tyre ☐

6.3 Find the missing letters to make a new word.

Word	Missing letter	Word	Missing letter	Word	Missing letter
1. –icket	t	4. custo–s	_____	7. p–ssport	_____
2. port–r	_____	5. su–tcase	_____	8. –uggage trolley	_____
3. baggage–eclaim area	_____	6. boardi–g pass	_____		

New word _ _ _ _ _ _ _ _ _ _ _ _ _ _

6.4 Put these vehicles in the correct category.

saloon car, yacht, hatchback, cabin cruiser, rowing boat, four-wheel drive, helicopter, convertible, oil tanker, cruise ship, estate car, ferry, jet plane

Air	Land	Sea

EXERCISES

7 COMMUNITY

7.1   Put the words in the correct boxes.

slot, water, stretcher, drip, ladder, hose, smoke, phonecard, ambulance, receiver, oxygen mask, fire extinguisher, paramedic

Fire brigade	Ambulance service	Phone box

7.2   What can you buy in these places? Connect the words.

1. optician's   a) stamp
2. stationer's   b) radio
3. sweet shop   c) tube of glue
4. travel agency   d) sunglasses
5. music shop   e) air ticket
6. electronics shop   f) piano
7. Post Office   g) bar of chocolate

7.3   Label the following items in the boxes provided.

letter, address,
postmark, postcode,
stamp, envelope

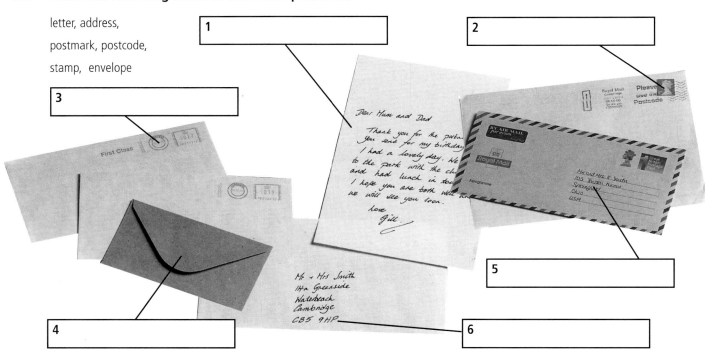

1

2

3

5

4

6

8 SPORT

8.1   Link the words to their sports type.

speed skating		basketball
surfing	water sports	cricket
sailing	individual sports	downhill skiing
golf	winter sports	rowing
archery	team sports	figure skating
football		diving

8.2   Football and rugby word soup. Find 8 words connected with football and rugby.

T	R	E	F	E	R	E	E	X
U	S	T	A	N	D	L	A	O
C	I	P	O	T	U	T	D	R
O	R	G	I	G	R	S	A	N
L	R	O	M	T	N	E	T	H
H	Y	A	W	A	C	W	C	E
U	T	L	O	D	E	H	A	G
W	A	I	S	H	R	P	U	A
Z	S	E	V	P	B	A	L	L
E	T	S	T	A	D	I	U	M

8.3   Answer these questions about sports equipment.

1.	Do footballers wear trunks?	No, they don't.
2.	Do rugby players wear pads?	
3.	Do boxers wear trunks?	
4.	Do footballers wear football boots?	
5.	Do batsmen wear goggles?	
6.	Do boxers wear goggles?	
7.	Do cyclists wear helmets?	
8.	Do roller-skaters wear helmets?	
9.	Do swimmers wear gloves?	
10.	Do scuba divers wear wet suits?	

9 ENTERTAINMENT

9.1 **Connect each hobby to one piece of equipment.**

photography   [knitting needles]   [telescope]   painting

knitting   [potter's wheel]   [binoculars]   astronomy

pottery   [brush]   [camera]   bird-watching

9.2 **Put the words in the correct box.**

pier   swimming costume

surfboard   windbreak

air bed   shell

beach towel   wave

sea   spade

bucket   sunglasses

Things you take to the beach	Things you find at the beach
_____	_____
_____	_____
_____	_____
_____	_____
_____	
_____	
_____	
_____	

9.3 **Find the missing letters to make a new word.**

Word	Missing letter	Word	Missing letter	Word	Missing letter
1. –amping	c	**4.** te–t	_____	**7.** pon–trekking	_____
2. ballo–ning	_____	**5.** na–ure reserve	_____		
3. r–cksack	_____	**6.** campe–	_____	**New word** _ _ _ _ _ _ _ _ _	

9.4 **What games are these? Unscramble the letters.**

1. sches _____
2. blbeasrc _____
3. pnlyooom _____
4. nomamgkacb _____
5. tdrsuagh _____
6. rdsca _____

9.5 **Look at these places to visit and fill in the missing words.**

park (2), home, wall, fair, gardens, shop

1. theme _____   3. craft _____   5. stately _____   7. book _____

2. city _____   4. botanical _____   6. safari _____

9.6 **Cross out the instruments in the wrong group.**

Strings	Woodwind	Brass
piano	flute	trombone
guitar	clarinet	saxophone
violin	saxophone	French horn
drum	recorder	trumpet
double bass	cymbal	tuba

10 THE ENVIRONMENT

10.1 Write the weather for each of these places.

Example: In Exeter it is foggy.

1. In London it is _____

2. In Manchester it is _____

3. In Newcastle it is _____

4. In Glasgow it is _____

10.2 Find the words for the pictures in the word soup:

H	N	H	V	B	X	G	O	S	E	N	Y	M	U	Y
W	I	J	V	E	O	C	M	K	S	E	Y	E	B	M
E	X	L	I	A	L	I	A	O	L	N	I	A	A	W
L	K	N	L	C	P	L	N	L	U	J	I	D	J	C
D	L	Y	K	H	K	V	A	Z	H	N	P	O	P	R
K	A	A	T	S	X	V	G	Y	J	K	T	W	P	M
I	E	M	W	A	T	E	R	F	A	L	L	A	E	P
P	T	X	O	G	O	M	C	A	V	E	E	R	I	H
S	L	C	B	S	T	P	A	E	Q	F	M	V	T	N
W	X	T	R	H	L	T	R	E	E	G	I	F	A	M
Y	R	D	E	S	E	R	T	C	S	E	G	Y	P	B
I	B	D	U	H	Z	Z	P	F	N	H	P	I	O	N
G	U	W	S	J	O	R	O	L	Q	P	I	N	N	Q
H	K	F	D	H	C	J	E	V	T	U	X	S	D	B
H	Q	L	P	U	X	O	T	B	B	J	S	J	Y	T

10.3 Write the names of the planets in the correct order from the nearest to the furthest from the sun.

Mercury	Saturn	Pluto
Earth	Venus	Neptune
Jupiter	Mars	Uranus

1. _____

2. _____

3. _____

4. _____

5. _____

6. _____

7. _____

8. _____

9. _____

KEY TO EXERCISES

1 PEOPLE

1.1
1. wake up
2. get up
3. have a shower
4. dry yourself
5. get dressed
6. go to work

1.2
1. Brad
2. Pitt
3. Male
4. Actor
5. 1106 Hollywood Drive, Los Angeles
6. CA 98554
7. 994-9872
8. American
9. 18/12/1963
10. Shawnee, Oklahoma
11. Married
12. Jennifer Aniston
13. No children

1.3
1. sister
2. father
3. aunt
4. grandmother
5. nephew
6. stepson
7. mother-in-law
8. half-sister
9. granddaughter
10. stepfather

1.4
1. single
2. married
3. widow
4. remarried
5. divorced

2 HOUSING

2.1
Kitchen
oven
washing-up liquid
spice rack
Bathroom
laundry basket
washbasin
Dining Room
dining table
napkin
Living Room
armchair
coffee table
settee/sofa
Bedroom
headboard
quilt
chest of drawers

2.2
1. bedroom
2. dining room
3. bathroom
4. garden
5. bathroom
6. kitchen
7. garden
8. kitchen
9. bedroom

2.3
1. Bedroom/bath
2. Bathroom/quilt
3. Living room/dishcloth
4. Garden/cot

2.4
1. fork
2. spoon
3. wine glass
4. dessertspoon
5. serviette
6. knife
7. soup spoon
8. salt
9. pepper
10. teaspoon

3 WORK

3.1
1. office
2. hospital
3. school
4. university
5. court
6. studio
7. bank
8. kitchen
9. restaurant

3.2
note appointments
file papers
offer refreshments
sign a letter
photocopy a document
send an e-mail

3.3
hole-punch 3
stapler 6
Sellotape 5
telephone 2
lamp 10
calendar 7
out tray 9
in tray 4
typewriter 1
pen 8

4 THE BODY

4.1
This man has got **short black** hair. He has got **big** eyes and a **long** nose. He has **long** eyelashes and thick **eyebrows**. His mouth is **small** and his **ears** are small too. He has a **long** beard and a **moustache**.

4.2
1. to frown
2. to sing
3. to hug
4. to pull
5. to push
6. to sit
7. to talk
8. to wave
9. to cry
10. to shake hands

4.3
1c
2d
3a
4e
5b

4.4
Head/Face
nose
ears
forehead
cheek
mouth
lips
Arm/Hand
wrist
palm
elbow
fingers
thumb
Leg
thigh
hip
ankle
calf
knee
kneecap
Body
waist
stomach
back

5 FOOD

5.1
Hello sir. What would you like to eat?
For the starter I would like **prawn cocktail**.
And for main course?
I would like **roast beef with Yorkshire pudding** and some **carrots** and **peas** for side vegetables.
Would you like a dessert?
Yes. Can I have **apple pie** please?
And to drink?
I would like **still mineral water.**

5.2
Meat
chicken
bacon
minced beef
pork chops
liver
Drinks
orange juice
beer
mineral water
Fish and seafood
cod fillet
lobster
crab
Dry goods and condiments
pepper
oil
sugar
cereal
vinegar
salt
pasta
rice
biscuits

5.3
The words to find are:
Across
DOUGHNUT
SWEETS
CRISPS
SANDWICH
HAMBURGER
Down
CONE
PIZZA
PEANUT
Diagonal
NAPKIN
COLA

6 TRANSPORT
6.1
1. track
2. platform
3. luggage compartment
4. bus stop
5. timetable
6. clock
7. ticket collector
8. train station

6.2
1. petrol cap
2. roof-rack
3. wing mirror
4. tyre
5. indicator
6. bumper
7. numberplate
8. windscreen wiper
9. exhaust pipe
10. bonnet
11. headlight

6.3
1. ticket
2. porter
3. baggage reclaim area
4. customs
5. suitcase
6. boarding pass
7. passport
8. luggage trolley
Spells the word: t-e-r-m-i-n-a-l

6.4
Air
helicopter
jet plane
Land
saloon car
hatchback
four-wheel drive
convertible
estate car
Sea
yacht
cabin cruiser
rowing boat
oil tanker
cruise ship
ferry

7 COMMUNITY
7.1
Fire brigade
water
ladder
hose
smoke
fire extinguisher

Ambulance service
stretcher
drip
ambulance
oxygen mask
paramedic
Phone box
slot
phonecard
receiver

7.2
1d
2c
3g
4e
5f
6b
7a

7.3
1. letter
2. stamp
3. postmark
4. envelope
5. address
6. postcode

8 SPORT
8.1
Water sports
surfing
sailing
rowing
diving
Individual sports
golf
archery
Winter sports
speed skating
downhill skiing
figure skating
Team sports
football
basketball
cricket

8.2
The eight words to find are:
Across
REFEREE
STAND
NET
BALL
STADIUM
Down
GOALIE(S)
Diagonal
PITCH
CROWD

8.3
2. No, they don't.
3. Yes, they do.
4. Yes they do.
5. No, they don't.
6. No, they don't.
7. Yes they do.
8. Yes they do.
9. No, they don't.
10. Yes they do.

9 ENTERTAINMENT
9.1
photography/camera
knitting/knitting needles
pottery/potter's wheel
painting/brush
astronomy/telescope
bird-watching/binoculars

9.2
Things you take …
1. surfboard
2. airbed
3. beach towel
4. bucket
5. swimming costume
6. windbreak
7. spade
8. sunglasses
Things you find …
pier
sea
shell
wave

9.3
1. camping
2. ballooning
3. rucksack
4. tent
5. nature reserve
6. camper
7. pony trekking
Spells the word:
c-o-u-n-t-r-y

9.4
1. chess
2. Scrabble
3. Monopoly
4. backgammon
5. draughts
6. cards

9.5
1. theme park
2. city wall
3. craft fair
4. botanical gardens
5. stately home
6. safari park
7. book shop

9.6
Strings – drum
Woodwind- cymbal
Brass- saxophone

10 ENVIRONMENT
10.1
1. In London it is sunny.
2. In Manchester it is cloudy and rainy.
3. In Newcastle it is cloudy.
4. In Glasgow it is snowy and cloudy.

10.2
Across
WATERFALL (9)
CAVE (2)
DESERT (4)
TREE (1)
Down
BEACH (10)
MEADOW (5)
POND (11)
Diagonal
HILL (12)
DAM (3)
LAKE (8)
MOUNTAIN (7)
PEAK (6)
VALLEY (13)

10.3
1. Mercury
2. Venus
3. Earth
4. Mars
5. Jupiter
6. Saturn
7. Urnus
8. Neptune
9. Pluto

GRAMMAR INDEX

The Autmobile Association (AA) **79** 19, 20

Ace Photography **107** 12

Addenbrooke's Hospital **38** 5, **40** 2–4, 16; **41** 13

Allsport **80** 1–4, 6–27, 35, 36–39; **81** 8–16; **82** 1–5, 7–14, 16, 17, F, 19, 20; **83** 3–6, 12–15, 21, 23–24; **84** 4, 7–12, 18–22, 29–32; **85** 7–19; **91** 19–21; **100** 40–44; **114** 31

The Anthony Blake Photo Library Ltd **8** 1–8, 11, 18; **55** 1–12, 22, 23; **56** 1–7, 31–37; **57** 1–3, 7, 8, 23, 25–28; **58** Shopping basket; **59** 1–10, 12–15, 19–28; **60** 1, 2, 4, 5, 8–18, 20–25; **61** 9, 12, 19–24, 26; **64** 1–6 , 8–13, 16–24

Mark Wagner – Aviation Images **70** 20, 21; **71** 12, 13

BAA Picture Library **65** 6–9; **70** A, 1, 3–7, 9, 13, 17, 18; **71** 14, 16–27

BBC **23** 2

Gareth Bowden **6** 1–21; **7** 11, 16; **8** 13, 19–22; **9** 1–3, 7, 8, 10, 23, 25–28, 32; **10** 1–4, 16–20; **11** 1–9, 19–22, 25; **12** 1–17; **13** 1–14, 16–24; **14** 6–9; **15** 3–7, 10–15, 21; **16** 1–17; **17** 1–3, 5–19, 21, 22; **19** 1–3, 6–10, 13, 14, 18, 19; **21** 4; **23** 8, 10, 16; **24** 3–12, 23; **25** 1–15; **27** 5, 6; **29** 2, 4–16, 21; **31** 1–36; **33** 16, 17; **34** 1, 3–13, 16–18, 21; **35** 1–19; **36** 1, 5–29, 31, 32; **38** 12; **43** 2–4, 8–23; **44** 1–12, 14–21; **45** 1–22; **46** 1–15, 17, 18, 21, 22; **51** 2–4, 7–12; **53** 5, 7, 18–21; **54** 7–12, 14–23; **56** 38–41; **65** 1, 2, 16, 20–23, 26–28; **66** 1–7, 17–23; **67** 1, 3–11, 13–35; **68** 1–5, 7–21; **69** 18, 19; **73** 1–7, 9; **74** 1–5, 8–10, 12, 13, 15–22; **75** 3–6, 8, 10–16, **76** 18–23; **77** 1–12, 14–27; **79** 1–3, 21–24; **86** 2–4, 8–15, 17–24; **87** 20; **91** 16–18; **111** 18; **114** 29, 30; **116** 1, 4

Getty Images (Photodisc) **53** 12

Priscilla Coleman **30** 5–12

Corbis **21** 11, 19, 20; **23** 3, 11; **28** 21; **33** 18; **53** 16, 17; **57** 5, 6; **65** 19; **72** 2; **75** 9; **78** 2–4, 7–10, 12, 14; **86** 7; **88** 12, 28; **94** 3; **102** 7; **110** 4

DIY Photo Library **21** 10, 12; **26** 6, 25, 26

Dorling Kindersley **5** 1–4, 6–9, 11, 12, 14–16; **8** 9, 10, 12; **9** 9, 11, 12, 29, 33; **10** 5, 23–25, 27; **11** 12, 23; **12** 18–20; **14** 10, 16, 19–21; **16** 25, 26, 28–30; **17** 23–29; **19** 11, 20; **27** 16; **28** 14, 16, 19; **30** 1, 3, 4, 13, 14; **31** 1–7; **32** 1–7; **33** 1–3, 5–7, 10–15; 19, 20, 22–25; **34** 14, 15, 19, 20; **38** 22; **40** 6, 13, 19, 20, 22; **41** 15, 16; **43** 1; **48** 22; **49** 5, 12–22, 24, 25, 30, 31, 35, 36; **50** 4; **51** 5, 6; **52** 25, 26, 31; **53** 8; **54** B; **55** 34; **56** 8–10, 15, 16, 30; **59** 11; **60** 6, 7, 19; **63** 1–5, 7–15, 17–28; **65** 3, 4, 13, 14, 18, 24, 25; **66** 9–11, 13, 15, 16; **71** 6, 11, 15; **72** 9, 10, 17,

18; **79** 17, 18 **79** 8, 9, 18, 19; **83** 7–11, 30–32; **87** 3, 4, 6–11, 18, 19; **88** 4, 5, 10, 11, 14–22, 24, 25; **89** 2–7, 9, 10; **90** 1–22, 24–28; **91** 1–4, 6, 7, 11, 12, 22–24; **92** 12, 14–20; **93** 5, 7, 10––14, 20, 21; **96** 12; **99** 15; **102** 3, 4; **106** 4, 10, 17–19, 28, 29, 31; **107** 4; **109** 1–9, 18; **111** 3, 5–17, 19–23; **112** Photographer 18–20; **114** 21, 22, 32; **115** 15, 16

Dyson **15** 20

Charlie Gray **7** 10, 12, 17–21; **19** 5, 15; **23** 1, 12; **27** 14, 15; **62** 18, 19, 26–29; **66** 8, 12; **73** 8; **88** 1–3; **115** 1, 2

Colorific **93** 8, 18, 21

GO **70** 2

Hart McLeod **5** 5, 10, 15; **7** F; **12** 21; **20** 1, 3–8; **21** 17; **26** 18, 21; **28** 8, 9, 15, 20; **30** 17; **40** 10; **42** 25; **53** 6, 16; **60** 3; **65** 17; 21–33; **70** 19; **73** 10; **75** 7; **79** 25–29; **84** 23–25; **89** 8; **100** 1–39, 45–48; **101** 1–24; **102** A, B; **103** 5–29; **104** Map; **105** Map; **107** 18–26; **108** 12; **109** 20–31; **110** 1–3, 5–18; **114** 27, 28; **116** 14–16

Hawkins Bazaar **18** 1–4

Helen Humphries **32** 10–22

JC Bamford Excavators Ltd (JCB) **28** 10, 13

The Galleries of Justice Museum **22** 9, 10

D McLeod **18** 6–16, 18–26

McDonald's Graphic Services **61** 6–8, 13–15

Phillips **37** 15

The Photographers Library **84** 5, 6; **107** 13

Pictor **4** 19; **7** 1–6; **33** 8; **38** 8; **50** 6, 7, 8, D, 20; **72** 12, 13; **82** 6; **85** 1, 2; **92** 9–11; **93** 1, 3; **99** 1, 2,

Planet Earth Pictures**72** 11; **94** 1; **95** 1–4, 7, 8, 10–15, 18; **96** 23, 28, 29, 31, 33; **97** 6, 7, 9, 10, 12–14, 17, 18, 22–26; **98** 1, 3, 11, 14–25, 27–31; **99** 3, 4, 6–8, 10–14, 16–21, 23–25; **106** 6–9, 13–16, 20–24, 32, 33; **108** 13–16, 22–30

Point to Point **21** 21;

The Post Office **76** 11–15

R & S Greenhill **102** 1, 3, 8

Reeve Photography **8** 14–17, 23–25; **9** 4–6, 13–22, 24, 30, 31; **10** 6–22, 26, 28–31; **11** 10, 11, 13–18, 24; **12** 22–24; **13** 15, 25; **14** 1–5, 11–15, 17, 18, 22, 23; **15** 1, 2, 8, 9, 18, 19, 22; **17** 4, 20; **18** 5, 17; **20** 9; **24** 1, 2, 13–22, 24–29; **26** 1–5, 7–17, 19, 20, 22–24, 27–34; **27** 11, 12; **28** 17, 18, 22–24; **29** 1, 3, 20, 17, 18;

32 23–29; **33** 4; **36** 4; **37** 1–14, 16–27; **39** 1–15; **40** 5; **41** 24; **42** 10–14, 26–29; **43** 5–7; **44** 13; **46** 16, 19, 20, 23; **47** 1–23; **48** 1–21, 23, 24, 27–30; **49** 1–4, 6–11, 23, 26–29, 32–34; **51** 1, 13–15, 17–27; **52** 1–10, 16–19, 30; **54** 13; **55** 13–21, 24–33; **56** 11–14, 17–29; **57** 4, 9–14, 24, 29; **58** 1–27; **59** 16–18, 29–35; **60** 26–31; **61** 1–5, 10, 11, 16–18, 25; **62** 1–17, 20–25; **63** 6, 16; **64** 7, 14, 15; **66** 14; **67** 2, 12; **73** 12–35; **74** 11, 14; **76** 1–10, 16, 17, 24–29; **77** Newsagent, 13; **79** 11; **80** 5, 32; **82** 15; **88** 23; **89** 1; **90** 23; **91** 5, 13–15; **92** 6; **93** 15, 16; **103** 1–4; **109** 10–17, 19; **111** 1, 2; **112** 1–16, woman on mobile phone, 21–23, ; **113** 1–15; **114** 1–20, 23–26, 31, 32; **115** 3–14; **116** 2, 3, 5–13, 17, 18

R.N.L.I. **72** 1

Robin Thompson **50** 3, 5

Royal Mail **22** 11

RSPCA Photolibrary **94** 1, 2, 4–16, 19; **95** 5, 9, 19–21; **96** 1–5, 13, 35; **97** 21; **98** 2; **99** 5, 9

Shout Picture Library **41** 12

Corbis Stockmarket **4** 28, 29; **19** 4, 21; **27** 9, 10; **34** 2; **41** 18; **48** 25, 26; **50** 1; **51** 16; **52** 32; **53** 2, 4, 15; **54** 1, 2, 4; **78** 5; **88** 6, 26, 27; **93** 4; **102** 5, 6, 9; **107** 69, 10, 14, 16

Tony Stone **53** 11

Telegraph Colour Library **4** 16–18, 20–27; **7** 7–9; **16** 20, 23; **19** 12, 17, 21; **20** 2; **21** 1–3, 5–9, 13–16, 18; **22** 1–8, 12–15; **23** 4, 7, 9, 13–15, 17–20; **27** 1–4, 7, 8, 13, 17; **28** 1–7, 11, 12; **30** 2, 15, 16; **33** 21; **36** 30; **38** 1, 2, 4, 7, 9, 11; **40** 1, 7, 12, 14, 15; **41** 4, 17, 19–23; **42** 1–9, 24, 32; **50** 2; **52** 11–15, 20–24, 27–29, 33, 34; **53** 1, 3, 9, 10, 13, 14; **54** 3, 5, 6; **57** 15–18; **65** 5, 10, 11, 15; **68** 6; **69** 20; **70** 8, 11, 12, 14–16; **71** 7–10; **72** 3–8, 14, 15, 16, 19–24; **74** 6, 7; **75** 1, 2; **78** 1, 6, 11, 13, 15; **79** 4–7, 10, 12–15; **80** 29–31, 33; **81** 1–4; **82** 18; **83** 1, 2, 16–20, 26-–29; **84** 1–3, 16, 17, 27, 28; **86** 1, 6; **87** 1, 2, 5 12–17; **88** 9; **91** 8, –10, 25; **92** 1–5, C, 7, 8, 13; **93** 2, 9, 17, 19; **94** 20–22; **95** 6, 16, 17, 22, 23; **96** 6–10, 14–22, 24–27, 30, 32, 34, 36; **97** 1–5, 8, 11, 15, 16, 19, 20; **98** 12, 13, 26; **102** 2; **106** 1–3, 5, 11, 26, 27, 30; **107** 1–3, 5, 7, 8, 11, 15; **108** 1–11, 17–21

SE Marshall & Co Ltd (Unwins) **16** 18, 19, 21, 22, 24, 27

Virgin Atlantic **71** 1–3

The Wellcome Trust **32** 8, 9; **38** 3, 6, 10, 13–21, 23; **40** 6, 8, 9, 11, 17, 18, 21; **41** 1–3, 5–11, 14; **42** 15–23, 30, 31

World Pictures **7** 13–15

ACKNOWLEDGEMENTS

Director
Della Summers

Senior Publisher
Laurence Delacroix

Project Editor
Karen Young

Design and photography
Hart McLeod

Production
Clive McKeough

Conversation activities
Liz Sharman

Exercises
Russell Stannard

Pronunciation Editor
Dinah Jackson

Pearson Education Limited
Edinburgh Gate
Harlow
Essex CM20 2JE
England
and Associated Companies throughout the world

Visit our website: http://www.longman.com/dictionaries

© Pearson Education Limited 2001, 2006
All rights reserved; no part of this publication may be reproduced, stored in a retrieval system, or transmitted in any form or by any means, electronic, mechanical, photocopying, recording or otherwise, without the prior written permission of the Publishers.

First published 2001
Second edition 2006
Fifth impression 2009

Words that the editors have reason to believe constitute trademarks have been described as such. However, neither the presence nor the absence of such a description should be regarded as affecting the legal status of any trademark.

ISBN: 978-1-4058-2798-0 (paper + audio CDs)

British Library Cataloguing-in-Publication Data
A catalogue record for this book is available from the British Library.

Set in Frutiger by Hart.McLeod, Cambridge
Printed in China
GCC/05

PRONUNCIATION TABLE

Symbol Consonants	Keyword	Symbol Vowels	Keyword
p	**p**ack	e	b**e**d
b	**b**ack	æ	b**a**d
t	**t**ie	i	happ**y**
d	**d**ie	iː	k**ee**per
k	**c**lass	ɪ	b**i**d
g	**g**lass	ɑː	f**a**ther
tʃ	**ch**ur**ch**	ɔː	c**a**ller
dʒ	**j**u**dge**	ɒ	p**o**t
f	**f**ew	ʊ	p**u**t
v	**v**iew	uː	b**oo**t
θ	**th**row	u	grad**u**al
ð	**th**ough	ʌ	c**u**t
s	**s**oon	ɜː	b**ir**d
z	**z**oo	ə	b**a**nana
ʃ	**sh**oe	eɪ	m**a**ke
ʒ	mea**s**ure	aɪ	b**i**te
m	su**m**	ɔɪ	b**oy**
n	su**n**	aʊ	n**ow**
ŋ	su**ng**	əʊ	b**oa**t
h	**h**ot	ɪə	h**ere**
l	**l**ot	eə	h**air**
r	**r**od	ʊə	t**our**
j	**y**et	eɪə	pl**ayer**
w	**w**et	aɪə	t**ire**
		ɔɪə	empl**oyer**
		aʊə	fl**ower**
		əʊə	**lower**

/ˈ/ shows main stress
/ˌ/ shows secondary stress
/ʳ/ means the /r/ sound is pronounced in American English but is usually not pronounced in British English, except at the end of a word when the word that follows begins with a vowel sound
/ə/ means that /ə/ may or may not be used